Creating a
Space to Grow

Creating a
Space to Grow

Developing your outdoor learning environment

Gail Ryder Richardson

 David Fulton Publishers

 **Learning through LANDSCAPES**

David Fulton Publishers Ltd
The Chiswick Centre, 414 Chiswick High Road, London W4 5TF

www.fultonpublishers.co.uk

First published in Great Britain in 2006 by David Fulton Publishers.

10 9 8 7 6 5 4 3 2 1

Note: The right of Gail Ryder Richardson to be identified as the author of this work has been asserted by her in accordance with the Copyright, Designs and Patents Act 1988.

Copyright © Gail Ryder Richardson 2006

British Library Cataloguing in Publication Data
A catalogue record for this book is available from the British Library.

David Fulton Publishers is a division of Granada Learning, part of ITV plc.

ISBN 1-84312-304-5

Typeset by FiSH Books, London
Printed and bound in Great Britain

Contents

Foreword

This book solves problems! Gail Ryder Richardson has successfully addressed the issue of the obstacles which stop babies and young children having access to the outdoor learning environment, and shown how these can be overcome. This is achieved not in the abstract but in step-by-step prompts and guidelines, based on real case studies. Practitioners can read about many situations – for example where settings have to share spaces with other groups or have only limited space for free flow play – and can be inspired to make a start on developing their own area. Follow or adapt the prompt sheets to your own situation and it all seems possible.

Two things are essential if young children are to have free access to an outside learning environment of quality. The first, of course, is space, directly leading to and from the indoor play room. The second prerequisite to worthwhile outdoor play is the knowledgeable and enthusiastic practitioner. This is the book to ignite that enthusiasm into action and deepen the knowledge of how to offer children the best environment for learning and the space to grow.

Marjorie Ouvry
Author of *Exercising Muscles and Minds:*
Outdoor Play and the Early Years Curriculum

Learning through Landscapes (LTL)

Learning through Landscapes (LTL) is the national school grounds charity, campaigning for positive outdoor learning and play experiences for all children in education and child care.

Since 1990 LTL has been undertaking research and evaluation, developing innovative projects and programmes, and providing training and support to raise awareness of the importance and special nature of the outdoors. Today, school and early years communities and those working on their behalf turn to LTL for guidance in developing and implementing improvements outside the classroom for the benefit of children.

LTL has been involved in the production of more than a hundred high quality publications, including books, videos and teaching resources. All are designed to help schools and early years settings realise the full potential of the outdoors – for healthy exercise, creative play, learning and making friends, and for putting children in touch with the natural world.

For further details on the work of Learning through Landscapes please visit our website at www.ltl.org.uk or write to Learning through Landscapes, Third Floor, Southside Offices, The Law Courts, Winchester SO23 9DL, or telephone 01962 845811.

Space to Grow

The Kent Space to Grow project has been a collaborative venture between Learning through Landscapes and Kent Early Years Development and Childcare Partnership (EYDCP) to address concerns about the quality of outdoor play within early years settings across Kent.

The aim of the project was to provide real examples of good practice, thus inspiring and motivating all settings in the county to develop their outdoor play provision. An inspirational publication based on case study material collected during the project, rather than a final report, was identified as an important output of the programme. *Creating a Space to Grow* will enable the findings and achievements of the project to be disseminated widely, thus being of benefit to early years practitioners in Kent and beyond.

The 22 settings involved in the project are listed below:

Bedgebury Junior School – Foundation Stage Unit, Goudhurst
Bell Wood Community Primary School, Maidstone
Bertie's Playgroup, Faversham
Bright Beginnings Day Nursery, Dartford
Ditton Church Pre-school, Ditton
Glebe House Day Nursery, Larkfield
Happy Faces Pre-school, Tonbridge
Highways at Hamstreet Kindergarten, Hamstreet
Little Acorns (Herne) Pre-school, Herne
Mary Sheridan Pre-school, Canterbury
MCNA Pre-school, Margate
Mongeham Primary School – Foundation Stage Unit, Mongeham
Northfleet Nursery School, Northfleet
Pipsqueaks Day Nursery, Queensborough
Saplings@The Sports Centre, Tunbridge Wells
St John's Primary School and Pre-school, Sevenoaks
St Martin's Pre-school, Folkestone
St Martin's Pre-school Group, Dover
Sticky Fingers Day Nursery, Ramsgate
Sunshine and Showers Nursery School, St Mary's Bay
Victoria Road Primary School, Ashford
White Oak Pre-school, Swanley

Acknowledgements

My sincere gratitude and appreciation goes to all those people who supported and encouraged me, firstly in the delivery of the Kent Space to Grow project and secondly throughout the writing of this book. In particular I would like to acknowledge the involvement of the following people.

Jan White, LTL's Senior Early Years Development Officer, and Jenny Middleton (formerly Kent's Senior Early Years Advisory Teacher) who worked together to develop the initial ideas for an outdoor project in Kent.

Peter Carne, Director of Operations at LTL, for his unshakeable confidence in my ability to deliver the project and write this book.

Alison Clark, from the Thomas Coram Research Unit, for her inspiration and encouragement.

Julia, Chris, Zoë, Steve, Jake and 'lovely Jenny' – the 'LTL in London' team who shared in the laughter and the tears – a big thank you to you all!

The Kent Early Years Advisory Team, particularly Julia Gouldson, Training and Quality Manager, and Karen Rolls, Senior Early Years Advisory Teacher.

And lastly, but most importantly, the children, parents, staff and management at all 22 Kent settings involved in the project and featured in this book – it couldn't have been written without you!

Introduction

This book is a testimony to the success of the Kent Space to Grow Project, a collaborative initiative between Kent's Early Years Development and Childcare Partnership (EYDCP) and Learning through Landscapes (LTL), a national charity that provides support to all those who value educational outdoor environments.

Since September 2003 Learning through Landscapes has worked with 22 early years settings in Kent. The settings include community pre-schools, Reception classes, an independent school, private pre-schools and day nurseries, as well as pre-schools funded by other bodies such as social services and health authorities. Some settings had reasonable access to a safe, secure outdoor environment and some had little or no outdoor space of their own.

The original aim of Kent's Early Years Development and Childcare Partnership was to help maintained and non-maintained early years settings to improve their outdoor play provision and practice. The Space to Grow project was funded by Kent EYDCP to develop demonstration settings in Kent across the range of early years provision. The settings involved were supported to identify their own barriers to offering effective outdoor learning, and to develop a range of relevant, copiable low-tech and affordable solutions that other early years providers could realistically transfer to their own situations. All the settings involved in the project made a commitment to provide access and share their practice with other settings, to inspire and motivate them to enhance their own provision.

The developments and improvements within the project focused on increasing children's access to outdoors, improving the quality of their play and learning experiences, and raising levels of confidence and enthusiasm for outdoor learning among early years practitioners.

The wider intentions of the project were

* to aid early years settings to move forward in their provision and practice for outdoor play towards an integrated indoor–outdoor experience for children

* to help settings in Kent meet the National Standards for Day Care and Childminding, the *Birth to Three Matters Framework*, the *Curriculum Guidance for the Foundation Stage* requirements and the Kent Quality Kitemark

* to find appropriate solutions to the limitations and barriers that prevent children from accessing and using the outdoors to its full potential

* to identify and develop management strategies for achieving high-quality outdoor provision

* to contribute to the development and dissemination of sound pedagogy for outdoor play in the early years

* to create demonstration sites in a range of settings to which all settings can relate, exploring the factors specific to different kinds of provision (e.g. pre-schools, private nurseries, nursery and Reception classes in schools) and disseminating good practice, enthusiasm and confidence

* to create and encourage a network of support and communication throughout the Kent early years sector

* to map out the process of change regarding outdoor provision in a wide range of settings and develop the process to make best use of the potential for children's well-being and development, family involvement and staff team effectiveness, to provide a model for change adoptable by others at the beginning of their journey.

Learning through Landscapes has been able to support each setting through this process of change and development. A key principle of Learning through Landscapes' work has been to promote a participative approach involving the whole community of each setting, and in particular the children.

Ideas for involving children in the development of their outdoor space

The settings involved in the Space to Grow project were encouraged to involve children in each stage of the process of developing their outdoor area. Each chapter includes all the techniques that were used in Kent and also incorporates other ideas that have been used successfully with very young children.

Each idea has been written up as a prompt sheet that identifies

* when to use the activity

* preparation and resources

* how to gather the information

* how to make sense of the information

* issues to consider.

There are ideas for each stage of the process to enable practitioners to involve children in 'Getting started', 'Thinking and planning', 'Making it happen' and 'Evaluating and enjoying'. However, consultation with, and involvement of, children is more likely to be successful if it is already embedded in the working practices of the setting. At the end of the book is a list of publications that are very useful background reading and will provide further information on techniques for consulting and involving young children.

The Kent Space to Grow project also provided an invaluable opportunity for working collaboratively with Alison Clark, a research officer at the Thomas Coram Research Unit of the Institute of Education, University of London. Alison Clark carried out a pilot research project, 'Spaces to Play', in Happy Faces Pre-school, one of the project settings in Kent. The research focused on using and extending the tools developed as part of the 'Mosaic approach', to explore young children's understanding and use of their outdoor play space. The resulting publication, *Spaces to Play: More listening to young children using the Mosaic approach* by Alison Clark and Peter Moss, explores how to listen to young children's views and experiences of their outdoor environment, in order to inform change. It describes the adaptation of the Mosaic approach to work with young children in outdoor spaces and demonstrates young children's competence in expressing their opinions on their environment. It discusses the challenges and future directions for practitioners and researchers in listening to young children.

All the Kent settings involved in the project have recognised the importance of improving children's opportunities for outdoor learning, and each group has worked hard over the course of the year to identify their priorities and find ways of overcoming the limitations of their own outdoor space.

Although Learning through Landscapes' direct involvement with the original 22 Kent settings has now finished, the work of the project continues within each group and across Kent. This book aims to inspire early years practitioners across the country who wish to develop their own outdoor environment. It shares a vision and ten core values for high-quality outdoor experiences developed by a consortium of early years professionals including representatives from Kent EYDCP. It highlights the requirements of the *Curriculum Guidance for the Foundation Stage* and the *Birth to Three Matters Framework* and considers the implications for practitioners and their role as outdoor educators.

The Learning through Landscapes approach to changing and developing the outdoor environment is described in detail. Illustrative case studies from the Space to Grow project focus on how the Kent settings identified and overcame the range of issues that hamper the provision of good outdoor play.

Up-to-date contact details for each setting can be obtained from Kent Early Years and Childcare Unit, Oakwood House, Maidstone, Kent ME16 8AE, by calling Kent Children's Information Service 08000 323230.

Alison Clark working with children at Happy Faces Pre-school

1 Why do children need to be outdoors?

The special nature of outdoors

The outdoor environment has features that are either different from indoors or cannot be offered on the same scale, or in the same way, indoors. Early years practitioners who recognise the special nature of outdoors acknowledge that it provides a significantly different and complementary environment for nurturing children's well-being and supporting their learning.

Freedom

The outdoors offers children many freedoms, which may extend or be different from the freedoms they can experience indoors:

* freedom to move around in a bigger space – vigorous activity, larger-scale play, or just 'feel' the space around them

* freedom to do things not possible indoors, e.g. riding bikes, leaping, puddle-jumping

* freedom to be more relaxed and inventive about exploring and using materials and resources – transporting, mixing, making a mess

* freedom to be boisterous and to make noise without disrupting others

* freedom to explore different ways of being, feeling, behaving and interacting – from active super-hero play to cloud watching.

Space

* Outdoors offers children additional space, upwards as well as sideways. The children can be at different levels, see things from a range of perspectives and have the sky as their 'roof'.

* The four 'elements' of earth, air, water and even fire (through outdoor cooking or role-play barbeques) need to be experienced directly.

* Outdoor space feels very different from indoors and includes light effects, air movements and temperature changes.

* Outdoors offers added space that encourages children to be more active and work on a larger scale across all areas of learning, and supports collaborative activity.

* Outdoors offers children a different mental and emotional space from that which exists indoors – it just *feels* different!

Contact with the natural world

* The outdoors offers children direct, extended and deeply engaging experiences with plants, mini-beasts, other animals such as birds, soil, sand and many other natural materials.

Whole-body, multi-sensory experiences

* Young children use their body to learn, by moving, doing and using all their senses. All babies and young children, and particularly those with sensory impairments, benefit from a multi-sensory environment.

* Children can be vigorous, boisterous and active for long periods. They can use their upper body and limbs, developing health, strength and co-ordination and enjoying and learning about what their bodies can do.

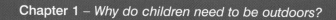

* The sounds and sights of the locality and community can be experienced then explored through outdoor play, especially in pretend and role-play.

Real experiences

* Real and direct experiences are easily offered outdoors through growing, experimenting with natural materials such as sand (on a large scale), running water and elements of the weather – rain, snow, frost, sunshine and so on.

* Children can gain real understanding of concepts such as volume and weight when transporting a barrow-full of sand, and distance or height when using the physical play apparatus.

Variety of spaces, places and perspectives

*   In addition to open space, outdoors can offer nooks and crannies among plants, climbing frames, playhouses and dens. Children can be enclosed (under or inside) or high up with a new perspective of looking down on their world.

*   Spaces can be active and provide large-scale opportunities, or can be places for calm, reflection, one-to-one interaction or the chance to be by oneself.

*   Spaces can be soft or hard or anything in between, giving a range of sensations through surfaces and planting.

Dynamic

*   Outdoors offers children the freedom to manipulate, change and be in control of their environment. Through the use of moveable, open-ended resources and materials, they can create new play environments.

*   The daily changes in the quality of the air, temperature and rainfall and the gradual changes through the seasons offer huge potential for real and direct experience and exploration – every day is different!

*   The uncertainty of daily changes and the surprise and excitement arising from spontaneous events, such as finding a ladybird or spotting a hot air balloon overhead, are all waiting to be captured and used to enrich children's experiences as they find out about their world.

Relationships with adults and other children

There is a different quality to the relationships a child can have outside with other children and with adults:

*   Children can choose to interact on a variety of activity levels or group sizes.

*   Working on a large scale or with bikes with trailers provides opportunities to co-operate, negotiate and collaborate.

✳ Adults can take time to sit and chat, get involved in play and exploration or simply stand back to observe and listen to children's play.

✳ It is often possible to engage children in activities outdoors that they are reluctant to participate in inside, for example mark-making or counting.

✳ Many adults find they are happy to tolerate higher levels of noise, mess and activity in the bigger, unrestricted space with no ceiling and have less concern about spillages or collision with obstacles.

✳ Children respond differently to adults outside. For example, some children who talk little inside are less inhibited outdoors.

Challenge and safety

✳ Outdoors provides experiences through which children can learn how to keep themselves safe and how to be aware of the safety of others.

✳ It offers children many ways to be adventurous and to challenge their own limits within a framework of safety provided by adults and the environment they have prepared.

(Adapted from Learning through Landscapes' *Early Years Outdoors* Curriculum Support, July 2004.)

A shared vision and core values for outdoor play

In Kent the EYDCP provides a network of support for all early years settings within the county. Through this ongoing contact with providers, Kent's early years advisory team identified that some settings were having difficulties in providing children with good access to a

stimulating outdoor environment and support from enthusiastic adults. The creation of the Space to Grow project was the first step towards addressing this concern. However, Kent EYDCP also joined other leading early years organisations and consultants with a professional interest in outdoor play to develop and endorse a shared vision of what good outdoor play should look like. See p. 10 for a list of those involved in this process.

Outdoor play – the shared vision for all young children

* All children have the right to experience and enjoy the essential and special nature of being outdoors.

* Young children thrive and their minds and bodies develop best when they have free access to stimulating outdoor environments for learning through play and real experiences.

* Knowledgeable and enthusiastic adults are crucial to unlocking the potential of outdoors.

Core values for high-quality outdoor experiences for young children

1 Young children should be outdoors as much as indoors and need a well-designed, well-organised, integrated indoor–outdoor environment, preferably with indoors and outdoors available simultaneously.

Outdoor provision is an essential part of the child's daily environment and life, not an option or an extra. Each half of the indoor–outdoor environment offers significantly different, but complementary, experiences and ways of being to young children. They should be available simultaneously and be experienced in a joined-up way,

Play is the means through which children find stimulation, well-being and happiness, and is the means through which they grow physically, intellectually and emotionally. Play is the most important thing for children to do outside and the most relevant way of offering learning outdoors. The outdoor environment is very well suited to meeting children's needs for all types of play, building upon first-hand experiences.

3 Outdoor provision can, and must, offer young children experiences that have a lot of meaning to them and are led by the child.

with each being given equal status and attention for their contribution to young children's well-being, health and stimulation and all areas of development.

Outdoor space must be considered a necessary part of an early years environment and be well thought through and well organised to maximise its value and usability by children and adults, and design and planning must support developmentally appropriate practice, being driven by children's interests and needs.

2 Play is the most important activity for young children outside.

Because of the freedom the outdoors offers to move on a large scale, to be active, noisy and messy and to use all their senses with their whole body, young children engage in the way they most need to explore, make sense of life and express their feeling and ideas. Many young children relate much more strongly to learning offered outdoors rather than indoors.

All areas of learning must be offered through a wide range of holistic experiences, both active and calm, which make the most of what the outdoors has to offer.

Outdoor provision needs to be organised so that children are stimulated, and able, to follow their own interests and needs through play-based activity, giving them independence, self-organisation, participation and empowerment. The adult role is crucial in achieving this effectively.

4 Young children need all the adults around them to understand why outdoor play provision is essential for them, and they need adults who are committed and able to make its potential available to them.

Young children need practitioners who value and enjoy the outdoors themselves, see the potential and consequences it has for young children's well-being and development, and want to be outside with them. Attitude, understanding, commitment and positive

of 'being', feeling, behaving and interacting; they have space – physical (upwards as well as sideways), mental and emotional; they have room and permission to be active, interactive, messy, noisy and work on a large scale; they may feel less controlled by adults.

The real contact with the elements, the seasons and the natural world, the range of perspectives, sensations and environments – multi-dimensional and multi-sensory – and the daily change, uncertainty, surprise and excitement all contribute to the desire young children have to be outside. It cannot be the same indoors, a child cannot *be* the same indoors – outdoors is a vital, special and deeply engaging place for young children.

6 Outdoors should be a dynamic, flexible and versatile place where children can choose, create, change and be in charge of their play environment.

thinking are important, as well as the skills to make the best use of what the outdoors has to offer and to effectively support child-led learning; the adult role outdoors must be as deeply considered as that indoors. Practitioners must be able to recognise, capture and share children's learning outdoors with parents and other people working with the child, so that they too become enthused. Cultural differences in attitude to the outdoors need to be understood and worked with sensitively to reach the best outcomes for children.

5 The outdoor space and curriculum must harness the special nature of the outdoors, to offer children what the indoors cannot. This should be the focus for outdoor provision, complementing and extending provision indoors.

Outdoor provision can, and should, offer young children an endlessly versatile, changeable and responsive environment for all types of play where they can manipulate, create, control and modify. This offers a huge sense of freedom, which is not readily available indoors. It also underpins the development of creativity and the dispositions for learning. The space itself and the resources, layout, planning and routines all need to be versatile, open-ended and flexible to maximise their value to the child.

7 Young children must have a rich outdoor environment full of irresistible stimuli, contexts for play, exploration and talk, and plenty of real experiences and contact with the natural world and with the community.

The outdoors offers young children essential experiences vital to their well-being, health and development in all areas. Children who miss these experiences are significantly deprived. Outdoors, children can have the freedom to explore different ways

Through outdoor play, young children can learn the skills of social interaction and friendship, care for living things and their environment, be curious and fascinated, experience awe, wonder and joy and become 'lost in the experience'. They can satisfy their deep urge to explore,

experiment and understand and become aware of their community and locality, thus developing a sense of connection to the physical, natural and human worlds.

A particular strength of outdoor provision is that it offers children many opportunities to experience the real world, have first-hand experiences, do real tasks and do what adults do, including being involved in the care of the outdoor space. Settings should make the most of this aspect, with connected play opportunities.

An aesthetic awareness of, and emotional link to, the non-constructed or controlled, multi-sensory and multi-dimensional natural world is a crucial component of human well-being, and increasingly absent in young children's lives. The richness of cultural diversity is an important part of our everyday world; this can and should be explored by children through outdoor experiences. Giving children a sense of belonging to something bigger than the immediate family or setting lays foundations for living as a community.

Young children should have long periods of time outside. They need to know that they can be outside every day, when they want to, and that they can develop their ideas for play over time.

High-quality play outdoors, where children are deeply involved, only emerges when they know they are not hurried. They need to have time to develop their use of spaces and resources and uninterrupted time to develop their play ideas, or to construct a place and then play in it or to get into problem-solving on a big scale. They need to be able to return to projects again and again until 'finished' with them.

Slow learning is good learning, giving time for assimilation. When children can move between indoors and outside, their play or explorations develop further still. Young children also need time (and places) to daydream, look on or simply relax outside.

8 Young children need challenge and risk within a framework of security and safety. The outdoor environment lends itself to offering challenge, helping children learn how to be safe and to be aware of others.

Children are seriously disadvantaged if they do not learn how to approach and manage physical and emotional risk. They can become either timid or reckless, or be unable to cope with consequences. Young children need to be able to set and meet their own challenges, become aware of their limits and push their abilities (at their own pace), be prepared to make mistakes, and experience the pleasure of feeling capable and competent. Challenge and its associated risk are vital for this. Young children also need to learn how to recognise and manage risk as life-skills, so as to become able to act safely, for themselves and others.

Safety of young children outdoors is paramount and a culture of 'risk assessment to enable' that permeates every aspect of outdoor provision is vital for all settings. Young children also need to feel secure, nurtured and valued outdoors. This includes clear behavioural boundaries (using rules to enable freedom), nurturing places and times outside and respect for how individual children prefer to play and learn.

9 Outdoor provision must support inclusion and meet the needs of individuals, offering a diverse range of play-based experiences.

Provision for learning outdoors is responsive to the needs of very active learners, those who need sensory or language stimulation and those who need space away from others – it makes provision more inclusive and is a vital learning environment. When children's learning styles are valued, their self-image benefits. Boys, who tend to use active learning modes more than girls and until they are older, are particularly disadvantaged by limited outdoor play.

All children need full access to provision outdoors and it is important to know and meet the needs and interests of each child as an individual. Young children react differently to the spaces and experiences available or created, so awareness and flexibility are key to the adult role. Observation and assessment (both formative and summative), and intervention for particular support, must be carried out outside. While it is important to ensure the safety of all children, it is equally important to ensure that all are sufficiently challenged.

10 Young children should participate in decisions and actions affecting their outdoor play.

Young children should take an active part in decisions and actions for outdoor provision, big and small. Their perspectives and views are critical and must be sought, and they can take an active role in setting up, clearing away and caring for the outdoor space.

The shared Vision and Values for outdoor play have been developed and endorsed by the following individuals and organisations:

Celia Burgess Macey, Goldsmiths, University of London
eds01cb@gold.ac.uk

Diane Rich, Rich Learning Opportunities
early-years@dianerich.co.uk

Early Education
www.early-education.org.uk

Early Excellence
jenny@earlyexcellence.com

Education Walsall
www.educationwalsall.org

Forum for Maintained Nursery Schools
www.early-education.org.uk

Gill McKinnon, Headteacher
High Yards Nursery School, Edinburgh
gill_mckinnon@breathemail.net

Grounds for Learning
www.gflscotland.org.uk

Helen Tovey, Roehampton University
www.roehampton.ac.uk/ses

Kent EYDCP
www.kent.gov.uk

Learning through Landscapes
www.ltl.org.uk

Margaret Edgington, author and consultant
edgington@madasafish.com

Marjorie Ouvry, author and consultant
ouvry@hervey.demon.co.uk

Mindstretchers (Scotland)
claire@mindstretchers.co.uk

National Day Nurseries Association
www.ndna.org.uk

Neath Port Talbot County Council
www.neath-porttalbot.gov.uk

Nursery World magazine
www.nurseryworld.co.uk

Pre-school Learning Alliance
www.pre-school.org.uk

Sightlines Initiative
www.sightlines-initiative.com

The curriculum outdoors

Both the *Birth to Three Matters Framework* and the *Curriculum Guidance for the Foundation Stage* place importance on children having good access and worthwhile experiences outdoors. Early years practitioners implementing these frameworks are required to acknowledge and respond to the explicit expectation that good quality learning experiences will be provided outdoors as well as indoors, for both babies and young children.

Birth to Three Matters Framework

Very young children have a natural fascination with the outdoors and yet many have very few opportunities to experience outdoor play in their home environment. Consequently, the provision of good quality outdoor experiences in early years settings is particularly important.

Outdoors can provide a place

where children become able to trust and rely on their own abilities, find out and become confident and competent in what they can do, valuing and appreciating their own abilities

(*Birth to Three Matters Framework: A Strong Child*)

where children can become sociable and effective communicators using their developing physical skills to make social contact, encouraging conversation, learning new words and meanings, describing, questioning and predicting

(*Birth to Three Matters Framework: A Skilful Communicator*)

in which children can explore, experiment, play and respond to the world creatively and imaginatively and make connections through the senses and movement to find out about the environment and other people

(*Birth to Three Matters Framework: A Competent Learner*)

where children can be active, acquire physical skills and gain control of their bodies, make decisions and choices and become aware of others and their needs

(*Birth to Three Matters Framework: A Healthy Child*)

The *Birth to Three Matters Framework* recognises that all children have, from birth, a need to develop learning through interaction with people and exploration of the world around them. When implementing this framework outdoors, practitioners should be aiming to:

support and encourage all children to enable them to gain confidence and to try new things;

(*Birth to Three Matters Framework: A Strong Child: Me, myself and I*)

find time to play, sing and laugh with young babies

(*Birth to Three Matters Framework: A Strong Child: Being acknowledged and affirmed*)

create areas in which children can sit and chat with friends or with staff, for example a shady outdoor den

(*Birth to Three Matters Framework: A Skilful Communicator: Being together*)

be available to explore and talk about things that interest young children outdoors and listen and respond to their questions, both serious and playful

(*Birth to Three Matters Framework: A Skilful Communicator: Listening and responding*)

thoroughly investigate the environment with children; for example, when outside consider how to shift leaves off a path, enlarge or 'disappear' a puddle, collect water dripping from a tap

(*Birth to Three Matters Framework: A Competent Learner: Making connections*)

provide opportunities for creative, physical outdoor experiences for babies such as bouncing, rolling and splashing

(*Birth to Three Matters Framework: A Competent Learner: Being creative*)

Birth to Three Matters: becoming a competent learner outdoors

What is a competent learner?

A competent learner is a child who uses all their senses to find out about whatever they come into contact with, including people, toys, clothes, furniture, books, flowers, grass, and anything else. Their curiosity leads them to understand that some things are predictable while others are not. Children who are competent learners watch the things that go on around them and they often imitate what they see and hear. They use materials imaginatively and creatively and begin to represent their ideas using marks. They are also investigators and explorers who try to find out how things work, and who create new uses for things. They are very active learners both physically, using their bodies, and mentally, using their minds.

Children become creative through exploration and discovery as they experiment with sound, media and movement. Creativity, imagination and representation allow children to share their thoughts, feelings, understandings and identities with others, using drawings, words, movement, music, dance and imaginative play.

How does the outdoors support very young children to become competent learners?

The outdoor environment offers endless stimuli to interest very young children, and a huge variety of materials and resources to feed their strong urge to explore and discover. The outdoors can provide wonderful experiences to support the development of the child as a competent learner. It is important that they have plenty of time outdoors every day, and essential that they can share their curiosity and delight with an interested, observant and tuned-in adult.

How can adults support the competent learner outdoors?

Observation of young children outdoors reveals how they use their bodies, senses and materials imaginatively and creatively. They have a noticeable fascination with natural materials as well as bought and found resources. Supportive adults offer many experiences to develop and extend young children's expanding imagination and creativity. For example, very young, non-mobile babies can be carried to different places in the outdoor area in order to be offered varied experiences: the moving leaves on a tree, or the smell of lavender bushes. As babies grow into toddlers they become more mobile and their exploration becomes more intentional. Careful observation of their interests and enthusiasms enables adults to support and encourage toddlers further in their endeavours.

Heads up, Lookers and Communicators (0–8 months)

Young babies respond to people and situations with their whole bodies. They are competent in observing and responding to their immediate environment.
Allow babies to lie, roll or crawl on different tactile surfaces, such as grass, rubber, stone, sand or snow, and provide babies with a selection of different materials, such as pebbles, shells or leaves, which allow them to make choices and explore with feet and hands. When playing with babies, sit closely or hold them, carrying them to explore together the objects or materials, talking to them about what they are doing.

Sitters, Standers and Explorers (8–18 months)

Babies' exploration becomes more intentional. Increasing mobility and language development enable them to find out and understand more about their world.

Provide materials that involve using all the senses and allow babies and toddlers to play both independently and as a group. Be aware of the ways in which babies communicate what they need. You can provide containers such as bags or buckets to allow them to transport materials from one place to another. Provide opportunities for babies to splash in puddles, tread in leaves or move in snow. Draw babies' attention to sounds such as splashing water, rustling leaves, wind chimes, birds or animals and traffic noises. Encourage them to listen and note the way babies show you they have understood by the way they respond verbally and non-verbally.

Walkers, Talkers and Pretenders (24–36 months)

Children's competence at moving, talking and pretending is increasingly evident and they show confidence in themselves.

Investigate the environment with children and discuss with them what resources they need and where they might find them. Encourage them to solve problems and make decisions for themselves, such as how to move the leaves from a path, enlarge a puddle or collect dripping water from a tap. Explore under stones and through collections of dead leaves for mini-beasts. Examine plants, twigs and stones and observe insects, butterflies and bees. Listen to what children say, describe and predict what they do, act as their interpreters and respond to their questions. As children learn to do things for themselves they gain confidence knowing you are close by, ready to support and help them if need be.

Movers, Shakers, Players (18–24 months)

Young children begin to show obvious pleasure in moving, communicating and learning through play.

Allow young children to experiment with combining materials such as sand, soil and water. Provide more opportunity for young children to transport materials from one area to another. Encourage young children to really investigate and talk about these experiences. Note how they use their senses and the creative ways in which young children use new language, sometimes combining words to make meaning.

(Originally published by Learning through Landscapes: *Early Years Outdoors* Curriculum Support, January 2005.)

Curriculum Guidance for the Foundation Stage

What experiences should children have outdoors?

Children need meaningful, engaging experiences outdoors that help them to develop in several areas of the curriculum at the same time in a natural way that draws on their own styles of behaving and learning. Outdoors is a place that supports progress towards early learning goals within all areas of learning. It offers children countless different experiences and, in many cases, these experiences are better or only possible outdoors.

Provision for Foundation Stage learning outdoors should give children opportunities to:

run, climb, pedal, throw...

* be physical on a large and a small scale

* enjoy a wide range of playful physical experiences

* take pleasure in movement and enjoy their bodies

be excited, energetic, adventurous, noisy...

* be energetic and boisterous

* be adventurous, with ideas as well as physically

* be uninhibited about being noisy and messy

talk, interact, make friends...

* use language to communicate and socialise

* explore ideas and have fun together

* play together, collaborate and co-operate

imagine, dream, invent...

* listen to, tell and act out stories

* engage in many kinds of pretend, fantasy and role-play

* explore behaving differently and 'being' someone else

create, construct...

* be imaginative, creative and expressive

* be inventive, constructive, de-constructive and find out how things work

* play in their own constructions and develop them

investigate, explore, discover, experiment...

* be curious and be fascinated

* experience and explore all kinds of materials and phenomena

* try out ideas and theories about how things behave or work

make music, express...

* make sounds and music with a range of items

* dance, chant rhymes and sing

* listen to and be influenced by a range of music

* express ideas, thoughts and feelings through a range of media using the scale and inspiration of the outdoors

find patterns, experience meanings...

* represent, make marks and see the written word

* experience and explore mathematical ideas and thinking

* have real experiences in order to really understand concepts

dig, grow, nurture...

* dig in sand, soil and mud

* grow a range of plants and witness growth, change and the seasonal cycles

* care for and nurture plants, wildlife and kept animals

hide, relax, find calm, reflect . . .

* be comfortable, calm, dream and enjoy being alone

* explore who they are and how they belong

* be themselves and play in their own way, at their own pace

have responsibility, be independent, collaborate . . .

* manage their own play and work together

* play and work with adults as equals

* change their play environment through flexible, versatile resources

(Adapted from materials originally published as Learning through Landscapes' *Early Years Outdoors* Curriculum Support, September 2004.)

Making links

Tables 1.1 and 1.2 provide an easy reference for early years practitioners wanting to make links between the *Birth to Three Matters Framework*, the *Curriculum Guidance for the Foundation Stage* and the development and use of their outdoor space.

Table 1.1 highlights the principles that underpin the *Birth to Three Matters Framework* and the implications for practitioners working with under-threes, and gives some examples of how the four Aspects and their four Components relate to outdoor learning.

Table 1.2 highlights the relevant principles and the requirements for teaching and learning outdoors within the Foundation Stage curriculum. It also looks closely at the role of adults outdoors, and considers how early years practitioners can put these principles into practice.

The role of adults as outdoor educators

The Shared Vision for high-quality outdoor play for all young children describes the adult as 'knowledgeable and enthusiastic' and 'crucial to unlocking the potential of the outdoors'. One of the key aims of the Space to Grow project was to increase practitioner confidence, motivation and enthusiasm for providing high-quality outdoor play for their children outdoors. However, throughout the country all early years practitioners are considering and developing their role outdoors. One of the best ways to begin this process is by observing what the children are currently doing; this provides useful insights and direct messages about their interests and enthusiasms. Through observation it is possible to determine what children know already and what experiences they need next.

Having observed children actively involved in outside play it is straightforward to plan what to do next. Other children may join in the play, and more materials brought in by the adults will develop the activity further. Focus on identifying the children's interests, and shape ideas for future sessions through the observations. Outline plans for future sessions should emerge out of the children's current play and activities. Through collaboration with the children, developed from ongoing observations, it will be possible to create a stimulating outdoor environment, a mixture of planned provision and child-initiated play that supports learning across all areas of the curriculum.

Effective outdoor educators:

* let the children take the lead in planning for outdoor play activities;

* support children by creating and developing an exciting and stimulating outdoor area which builds on their interests;

* take time to discover a completely different side to the child who has remained quiet and introverted indoors;

* welcome the increase in noise levels and conversations as children enjoy the freedom of outdoors;

* join in with the children – play alongside them, ask questions and introduce new ideas, language and skills;

19

* take a genuine and enthusiastic interest in the children's own world of outdoor play;

* have fun and enjoy being outside;

* value the impact of exercise outdoors on the health and well-being of both the children and the adults.

(Adapted from materials originally published as Learning through Landscapes' *Early Years Outdoors* Curriculum Support, March 2005.)

Table 1.1 Making links between the Birth to Three Matters Framework and provision for learning outdoors.

Principles which underpin the *Birth to Three Matters Framework* (from the Introductory Booklet pp. 4–5)	The implications for early years practitioners	Planning and resourcing reference
Parents and families are central to the well-being of the child.	Plan time to talk in depth to parents about how their young baby communicates needs.	A Skilful Communicator (Making Meaning)
Relationships with other people (both adults and children) are of crucial importance in a child's life.	Discuss with staff/parents how each child responds to activities/adults/peers and build on this to plan future activities and experiences for each child.	A Strong Child (Being Acknowledged and Affirmed)
A relationship with a key person at home and in the setting is essential to young children's well-being.	Plan for key people to be with babies and children to create opportunities for snuggling in.	A Strong Child (A Sense of Belonging)
Caring adults count more than resources and equipment.	Plan opportunities for talking together in quiet places outdoors.	A Skilful Communicator (Being Together)
Babies and young children are social beings; they are competent learners from birth.	Plan opportunities for exploring interesting objects and resources together, e.g. leaves, mini-beasts, water, the view out.	A Competent Learner (Making Connections)
Learning is a shared process and children learn most effectively when, with the support of a knowledgeable and trusted adult, they are actively involved and interested.	Flexible arrangements of equipment and materials for babies and children can be used in a variety of ways to maintain interest and challenge.	A Healthy Child (Keeping Safe)
Children learn where they are given appropriate responsibility; allowed to make errors, decisions and choices; and respected as autonomous and competent learners.	Plan opportunities that allow children to make and discuss their choices with regard to activities, people and visits.	A Skilful Communicator (Making Meaning)
Children learn by doing rather than being told.	Provide materials that encourage young children to pretend without adult intervention; e.g. a real telephone, an old camera, cooking equipment, blankets and tents outdoors.	A Competent Learner (Being Imaginative)
Schedules and routines must flow with the child's needs.	Recognise that outdoor provision presents rich choices for babies and children and include this in planning, e.g. streamers, bubbles and windmills in a 'windy day' box.	A Healthy Child (Healthy Choices)
Young children are vulnerable. They learn to be independent by having someone they can depend on.	Plan specific opportunities for all children to build secure relationships with key adults.	A Strong Child (Being Acknowledged and Affirmed)

Source: Early Years Outdoors. 'Outdoor Play' in the *Birth to Three Matters Framework*

Source: Early Years Outdoors Play in the Foundation Stage Curriculum Guidance. Quotes from Curriculum Guidance in italics.

22

Guiding Principles for early years education, page 11	Requirements for teaching and learning outdoors	What are the implications for early years practitioners?	FSCG page ref
To be effective, an early years curriculum should be carefully structured ... *Well-planned play, both indoors and outdoors, is a key way in which young children learn with enjoyment and challenge*	This principle requires practitioners to plan a carefully structured curriculum that provides rich and stimulating experiences through planned and purposeful activity that provides opportunities for teaching and learning, both indoors and outdoors	*We need to plan experiences that are relevant, imaginative, motivating, enjoyable and challenging* / We need to make effective use of unexpected and unforeseen opportunities for children's learning that arise from everyday events and routines / *We need to make good use of outdoor space so that children are enabled to learn by working on a larger, more active scale than is possible indoors*	15 11 25
No child should be excluded or disadvantaged / For children to have rich and stimulating experiences the learning environment should be well planned and well organised	These principles require practitioners to plan a learning environment, indoors and outdoors that encourages a positive attitude to learning through rich and stimulating experiences and by ensuring each child feels included	*We need to include the local community and environment as a source of learning* / We need to encourage children to make choices and develop independence by having equipment and materials readily available and well organised / We need to provide resources that inspire children and encourage them to initiate their own learning / *We need to give children the space they need for their activities*	14
There should be opportunities for children to engage in activities planned by adults and also those that they plan or initiate themselves / Well-planned, purposeful activity and appropriate intervention by practitioners will engage children in the learning process	These principles require practitioners to provide a relevant curriculum that is carefully structured with well-planned activities and appropriate intervention	We need to plan our time well so that most of it is spent working directly with children / *We need to accommodate the different ways children learn* by planning for the same learning objective in a range of different ways / We need to help children consolidate their learning by revisiting the same activities many times / We need to plan sessions to include both adult and child planned activities with uninterrupted time for children to work in depth / *We need to enable children to become involved by planning experiences which are mostly based on real life situations [and] allow time for sustained concentration*	16 15
Practitioners must be able to observe and respond appropriately to children	This principle requires practitioners to observe children and respond appropriately to help them make progress	We need to make systematic observations and assessment of each child's achievements, interests and learning styles / We need to use these observations and assessments to identify learning priorities and plan relevant and motivating learning experiences for each child	16

Table 1.2 Making links between the Curriculum Guidance for the Foundation Stage and provision for learning outdoors.

2 Getting started

Changing and developing the outdoor environment

Learning through Landscapes advocates that co-operation and involvement lie at the heart of any plan to improve the outdoor environment: For maximum success, outdoor play projects require the combined efforts of everyone: teaching and non-teaching staff, governors/management committee, children and parents.

The process of change and development is based on three underlying principles. Changes must be

* holistic: involving consideration of the whole site, the whole child, the whole setting community (i.e. children, parents, staff, management) and the whole curriculum (i.e. learning experiences that are planned or unplanned, as well as those that are child-initiated or adult-directed);

* participative: experience has shown that the most successful developments have involved children with adults in all aspects of the project, including the development of ideas, decision-making, helping with practical projects, and longer-term maintenance and evaluation of the project;

* sustainable: as well as aiming to use sustainable principles and practices, consideration must be given to the management and maintenance of the outdoor space in the longer term. This will ensure that what has been initially achieved continues to develop and be of benefit to others in the future.

These three principles provide the context for making changes to the use of outdoors. However, Learning through Landscapes has also developed a step-by-step process to guide and support early years practitioners wishing to develop their outdoor spaces. The following chapters look at that process in detail and gives examples of how it was implemented in Kent.

Telling people about the project

Getting everyone enthusiastic and committed to the project is a very valuable first step. It ensures that the responsibility for the project does not fall solely on a few individuals and enables identification of people with useful skills. The chair of the management committee at Little Acorns (Herne) Pre-school recognised that the commitment of the staff, the committee and the parents was essential to ensure the progress and success of any outdoor developments. So, before formally joining the project, the committee canvassed for parental support at their Annual General Meeting. Having established that parents were in favour of becoming part

The outdoor area at Ditton Church Pre-school at the beginning of the project.

...and after six months hard work!

of the Space to Grow project, the chair and supervisor arranged for a presentation about the project to be shared with staff to inspire them with ideas and to show what could be achieved. Spending time on these preliminary meetings ensured that everyone was aware and committed from the outset.

In March 2004 Learning through Landscapes conducted a six-month review of the Space to Grow project, to identify what had been learnt and achieved and to provide a focus for the remainder of the project. All those involved in the review meetings were asked to complete a timeline showing their personal highs and lows and the identifying factors attributable to these feelings. Table 2.1 shows a summary of the comments made during the review. One of the key messages to come out of this review highlights the importance of involving others and sharing the workload.

There are many effective ways to canvass support and ensure that everyone is involved in the process. Examples include

* talking with the children at Circle Time

* giving a presentation to all staff and the management team

* holding an information evening for parents and the local community

* sending a publicity flyer home with each child

* mounting a display

* involving the local media

* including an article or an advertisement in the parents' newsletter or on the setting's website.

Table 2.1 Kent Space to Grow Project six-month review: summary of positives and negatives

Positive factors and influences	Negative factors and influences
* Being part of something bigger	* Delays
* Inspiration from other places/people	* Unrealistic timescales
* Support from a wider body of people – parents, management, staff	* Lack of support from parents, staff
* Positive feedback from others – staff, children, parents	* Other demands on time
* Having some initial successes	* Extra workload
* Getting started	* Unreliable contractors
* Visual changes	* Costs – spiralling/unforeseen/underestimated
* Noticing the impact on children's learning/behaviour/development	* Red tape from regulatory bodies
	* Weather
	* Concerns about vandalism and security
	* Unrelated factors, e.g. staff sickness, Ofsted inspections

The Kent settings recognised the need to enthuse parents about the benefits of regular access to outdoor provision. Those settings that successfully shared with parents the benefits of learning through play outdoors found that, as parents became increasingly skilled at recognising the learning that was taking place outdoors, they became more interested in their children's activities in that space.

Identifying who can help

It is useful to conduct a skills audit in the early stages of the project to ascertain who might be able to do what and to encourage as many people as possible to get involved. The list below is not exhaustive but it includes some of the skills that may be needed as the project progresses:

* gardening

* designing

* art work

* letter writing

* fundraising

* catering

* carpentry

* crèche organisation

* book keeping

* first aid

* computing skills.

Try a range of approaches to identify the people with the right skills. Ditton Church Pre-school had a very positive response to a letter they sent to parents and friends of the pre-school and members of Ditton Church (Figure 2.1). However, other settings had more success by making a direct and personal request to individuals. For example, Sunshine and Showers Nursery School had success in persuading the regulars at their local pub to support their project plans. The Foundation Stage staff at Bedgebury Junior School held a very successful coffee morning for parents, to provide information about the project. Key members of the school community were also invited; for example, a member of the team responsible for maintaining the school grounds, and the bursar. This ensured that the whole school community was aware and involved from the outset and helped secure ongoing support for the project.

Bedgebury Junior School Foundation Stage play area

July 2003

Dear Parents/Friends of Ditton Church Pre-school/ Members of Ditton Church

I have great pleasure in announcing that we are 1 of 15 schools from 150 applications that have been selected to be part of an **Outdoor Play Project** led by **Learning through Landscapes** and **Kent Early Years Childcare Unit.**

Funding will be available for use to renovate our rear garden to develop a safe, secure and stimulating **outdoor play** and **learning area**, where all aspects of the foundation stage curriculum can be provided.

We need the following from everyone.

* **Ideas** – What would you like to see in the garden?

* **Your children's ideas** – What would they like to see in their garden?

* **Your knowledge and advice** – Have we any builders/gardeners/carpenters that would help with advice, practical help or lend equipment.

* **Your muscle** – we do need to have an element of voluntary work for the funding to be fully released – can you spare an hour or two over the holidays to help clear the garden?

* **Your contacts** – Do you know anyone that could be helpful in a project like this?

We would all be very grateful if you could help in any way as we are thrilled to be part of such a great project that will benefit all that use the Church Centre.

Figure 2.1 Letter sent from Ditton Church Pre-school

Co-ordinating the project

It is very useful to establish a group of interested people to co-ordinate the project as it progresses. This project team can make and review plans, delegate tasks, organise events, and provide a focus for feedback, discussion and decision-making. It is a good idea to allocate specific roles to team members so that each person has a clear responsibility for action and feedback.

Members of the project team could include

* senior staff, for example pre-school leader, head teacher, officer-in-charge

* teaching staff

* non-teaching staff, for example caretaker/grounds person, midday supervisors, administrative staff

* management, for example a pre-school committee member or school governor

* parents, who will also be able to contribute valuable insights into their child's perspective

* as appropriate, external organisations, for example a representative from the EYDCP, volunteer groups, or environmental organisations.

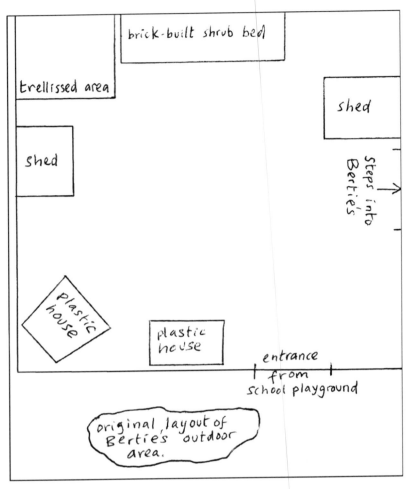

Figure 2.2 Bertie's Playgroup – Plan of the Outdoor area

Involving everyone in developing the project plans

A base plan showing the external area is very useful when planning improvements. It can be used to map what exists on the site at present. At Bertie's Playgroup in Faversham the staff created a plan of the outdoor area and highlighted the existing features (Figure 2.2). This plan was then used as the starting point for consultations and planning regarding the future use of the space.

Aim to record everything on the plan: trees, buildings and fences, access routes, cultivated areas, seating and any existing fixed play equipment. Include the features that are to be kept and those that may be removed. An enthusiast within the setting can draft scale site plans, or it may be possible to obtain plans from the local authority. If landscaping changes are being made, more detailed information will be required about the location and existence of underground and overhead services, for example water, gas, electricity, telephone, drains. This information is obtainable from the relevant local utility companies.

Once the plan of the existing features has been completed, keep one copy as a master version, and make several copies to use as working documents.

Involving staff

Gathering the views of staff is an important stage in the development of the project. Asking staff to identify the positive and negative aspects of the outdoor area often reveals differences of opinion and raises some interesting points for discussion. For example, Table 2.2 shows that the large outdoor space is seen as positive by some staff who recognise the freedom it offers children. However, it is also seen as a negative feature by staff with concerns about maintaining appropriate levels of supervision. Discussion and resolution of these issues is an integral part of the process of developing the use and management of the outdoor space.

Table 2.2 *Examples of typical comments from staff about the outdoor environment*

Positive aspects	Negative aspects
* 'Safe and secure' * 'Variety of surfaces including tarmac and grass' * 'Big fixed equipment' * 'Plants and trees' * 'Large space children can go anywhere' * 'Children love being outdoors'	* 'Bike play lacks purpose' * 'Sheds are not in a good position' * 'Static equipment has less flexibility and play value' * 'Wet grass – gets muddy, have to keep children off it' * 'Supervision difficult – can't see all the children all the time' * 'Have to be outdoors too long – gets cold in the winter'

Before making any changes it is important to find out how the outdoor space is used at present to support children's learning. Ask staff to consider how they would like to extend the use of outdoors in the future. Analyse curriculum plans to identify which aspects of learning take place outdoors, when and where, as well as any gaps in the existing provision.

Case study 2.1: Gathering the views of staff
Victoria Road Primary School, Ashford.

The Reception children at Victoria Road Primary School in Ashford use a mobile classroom sited at the edge of the school playground. The teaching staff were very keen to provide them with access to an outdoor environment for learning, and prior to the project they had already reclaimed a small unused courtyard behind the mobile classroom. This allowed small groups of children to take turns to have access to outdoors. However, it was not big enough to accommodate all children and support outdoor learning across all areas of the Foundation Stage curriculum.

Developing the Reception children's use of the large playground during lesson time was being considered as an option for improving their access to outdoors. However, consultation with staff revealed their concerns about using this space. The key issues identified by staff focused on the following aspects:

* The playground in its current state was a bleak and barren environment.

* The playground did not support a wide range of experiences to nurture children's knowledge and understanding of the world; in particular there were few opportunities for children to experience the natural world

The provision for children's creative development would be ineffective since the playground lacked features to support this aspect of children's learning The views of staff were noted and provided a vital insight into the problems that needed addressing through the project.

The first step towards curriculum development is a review of the existing possibilities for learning. By taking stock of everything that is already present in the outdoor space, including features such as plants, surfaces, walls and raised areas, staff will have a clearer awareness of the existing potential for supporting children's learning. For example, walls can be used for large-scale painting activities, traverse climbing, chalking and exploration of texture. See Figure 2.3.

This review will also help the project team identify the issues that are currently preventing staff from making the best use of the outdoor space; for example, difficult access, shared use of the space, lack of shade. Record

This part of the audit is to help you evaluate the PHYSICAL and AESTHETIC qualities of the outdoor space you have access to.

Auditing the physical environment	What happens now? What is the existing provision? Who is using it? What experiences do children currently have? How are adults involved?	How well does this work for us? What is working well? What is less effective?	What limits this? What makes it difficult, limits or prevents us from improving this aspect? i.e. space / staffing / cash / resources / H&S / other?	How could this be made better? What could we do to develop children's use of our outdoor space? i.e. space planning / staff development / developing resources / other?
How easy is it for our children to move between indoors and outdoors?	Mostly free-flow. 3 steps + adult support	Summer – Easier. doors + steps in winter.	transition area awkward to access. H+S – steps and door.	ease of accessing coats – poss. relocate.
How easy is it to set up/clear away equipment and activities outside?	2 sheds—adult access all activities ∴ adult initiated	variety of equip. difficult to set up.	space + access to sheds.	child access to resources. more variety. Don't require equip.
Do we have adequate, safe, secure outdoor storage areas?	2 sheds – safe and secure.	safe + secure.	could be bigger with better access.	get more adequate storage.
Do we have a variety of surfaces, textures, colours and shapes?	tarmac. coloured plastic equip	can use all year. Is not used effic. all year. Lack of variety.	ideas, resources	provide more of...
Do we have a secure and attractive site boundary?	secure fence boundary.	more could be made of the boundary as a resource.	cash + resources.	Could be made more attractive.
Do we provide a special area for babies and toddlers?	N/A my		N/A	
Do we have interesting views out of our site?	into school & ground. Some green & trees.	children can see through fence – see their siblings.		
Have we any seating areas?	the plastic picnic bench.	is portable but is plastic + limited.	space, ideas!	ask children where they would like to sit.
Do we make the most of our planted/green spaces?	Planted border pots all adult initiated/tended.	have space for planting no trees/child gardening opportunities.	knowledge + ideas.	input from green-fingered person!
Do we have any shade or shelter?	No shade/shelter	child can't play out if too hot/raining.	cash + resources, ideas.	Shelter from rain. Shade from sun.
How are we catering for children's physical play needs?	All ch'n have access of resources. + use of adults' support	child'n make use of equip. Not enough equip climbing/jumping etc.	resources	Plan for all aspects of physical play.

Figure 2.3 Auditing the physical environment – Bertie's Playgroup

the outcomes of these discussions with staff for future reference as the project progresses. Learning through Landscapes provides a useful audit sheet activity as part of its support for members of *Early Years Outdoors*. Several settings made good use of the audit activity to review their outdoor space. At Glebe House Day Nursery the owner commented, 'The audit was very useful, it seemed hard at first but once we had completed it, it really helped us formulate our plans.'

If the outdoor space is not currently being used at all, discuss with staff what initial changes would enable them to begin to support Foundation Stage learning outdoors. Their response may focus on practical issues, for example inadequate fencing, or lack of resources. There may be organisational difficulties related to deployment or storage. Alternatively, the poor use of outdoors may be linked to a lack of confidence among staff in relation to their own role outdoors. At St Martin's Pre-school Group, Dover, staff and children were already making some good use of outdoors, however their willingness to initiate further improvements to their outdoor space was hampered by uncertainties about the group's long-term viability (see Chapter 4, Case study 4.13).

Whatever the concerns, the project team will need to support staff to identify the underlying reasons and then make effective use of this information to guide the project focus.

Involving children

Equally important is an evaluation of children's use of the existing space. If the consultation process is meaningful to them, children will be able to provide valuable input to the project. However, to be truly effective, the skill of listening to and consulting with young children must be embedded in everyday practice. If adults go through the motions of listening yet do not enable children to make a difference to the direction of the project, the consultation process will be meaningless and frustrating. Children will quickly be discouraged from expressing their views if they feel that their participation has neither been taken into account nor respected. At the end of each chapter the strategies and ideas used within the Space to Grow project for gathering the views and perspectives of children are set out in a series of prompt sheets. The final section of the book includes recommendations for essential further reading for further information and a greater understanding of useful techniques.

As part of the Space to Grow project, the settings were encouraged to involve children in the development of the outdoor space. Settings were asked to find out how children felt about their existing outdoor space, and identify how they used it at the time. The Reception children at Victoria Road Primary School were asked what they liked and disliked about their existing outdoor space. (See Figure 2.4.)

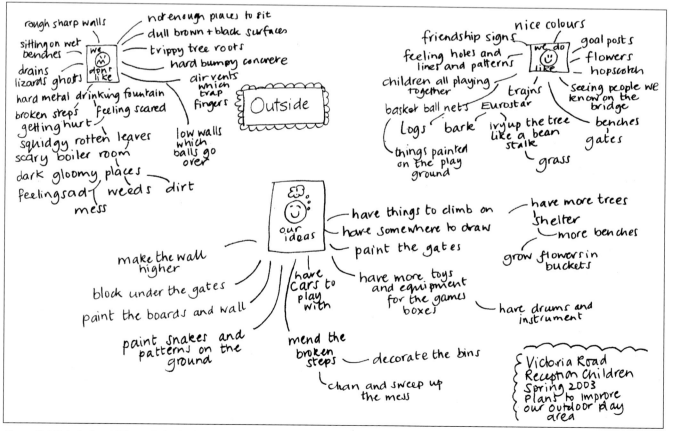

Figure 2.4 Victoria Road Primary School: children's likes and dislikes

Settings were asked to observe children and collect information on the types of activities the children engaged in while outdoors – both adult-planned and child-initiated.

Children outdoors at Happy Faces Pre-School

They noted how children used the space, where they went and how all these play activities impacted on each other. They considered whether children had a wide range of outdoor opportunities and experiences over time. They reflected on whether any of these experiences were particularly important for the children attending, and therefore a priority for further development.

In several settings, children were given disposable cameras to take photographs of the outdoor places that were important to them. Once developed, these pictures were used to stimulate further discussion. Each child talked about their photographs, made comments and answered questions about their views on future changes to the space. (See Case study 2.2.)

Case study 2.2: Gathering children's perspectives Happy Faces Pre-school, Tonbridge

The Kent Space to Grow project incorporated a pilot research project 'Spaces to Play'. The Thomas Coram Research Unit carried out this pilot study at Happy Faces Pre-school. The children worked with the researcher to explore their understanding and use of outdoor provision, in order to inform the process of change to their outdoor play space. The pilot used the Mosaic approach, which combines the traditional research tools of observation and interviewing with participatory methods, including the use of cameras (Clark and Moss 2001). Children were given single-use or cheap re-usable cameras and were asked to 'take photographs of what is

important here'. The children's choice of subject for their pictures was wide ranging and reflected their different priorities. For example, some children focused on taking pictures of their friends in different parts of the garden, whereas other children concentrated on capturing images of their favourite pieces of equipment. Many children included images of the sky and the perimeter fencing, this recurring theme emphasised to adults how children's outdoor experiences were being dominated by the imposing fencing.

The developed photographs were discussed at length and these conversations provided further insights. Individual children chose particular photographs of their outdoor space to make into a book and these books were shared with others in the setting. The work with cameras provided invaluable information about children's perspectives of their space and enabled the researcher and staff to reflect on the direction for future developments in the pre-school.

Alison Clark discussing photographs at Happy Faces Pre-School

At Sticky Fingers Day Nursery staff came to realise the importance of asking children what they wanted to **do** outdoors rather what they would like to **have**. Children's wish list in response to the second question included 'a slide up the clouds' – a lovely idea but not easily provided in any setting! (See Case study 2.3.)

Case study 2.3: Sticky Fingers Day Nursery: Gathering ideas from children

The staff at Sticky Fingers Day Nursery were keen to gather ideas from children as part of their initial consultations about the development of the garden. The children were asked two questions and their answers illustrate the importance of asking the right question in the first place.

When asked what they would like to have in their garden their responses included the following ideas:

'A big big trampoline'

'A really big climbing frame with lots of things on it'

'A slide up to the clouds'

'Swings and a see-saw'

'A house or a bus or a train or anything with things you can sit on and pictures on the wall'.

Children were also asked what they would like to be able to **do** outside. Their responses included the following comments:

'Run around'

'Chalk on the floor'

'Just play in it'

'Have fun'

'Play hide and seek with tents'

'Do digging and planting'.

The staff realised that children's responses to this question provided a much more useful starting point for future developments in the garden and included these ideas in their initial planning for the outdoor environment.

In some settings, where children were not currently going into the space earmarked for development, the staff had a harder challenge. How were they to consult children in a meaningful way about outdoors if it was not currently accessible? In Ditton Church Pre-school (see Case study 2.4), where the garden was not currently used at all, staff and parents took children to an alternative outdoor environment to observe their interests. The visit provided staff with a wealth of information about children's enthusiasms, which was then incorporated into their own project plans.

Case study 2.4: Involving children
Ditton Church Pre-school, Ditton

Ditton Church Pre-school is situated in the Church Centre in Ditton village. It has been open for nearly four years and originally the only outdoor space available to staff and children was the car park at the front of the Church Centre. This enabled some outdoor play, for example with tricycles and balls, but it was not a suitable space for supporting the full range of learning experiences outdoors. However, in July 2003 the pre-school were given permission to use part of the garden at the rear of the building. A tour of the space revealed an enormous task ahead – the garden was totally overgrown with nettles and brambles. Rubbish would have to be removed, fences installed and storage repositioned before the staff could begin to think about using the garden to enrich children's learning within the Foundation Stage curriculum.

At the beginning of the project one of the most important stages was to identify the children's priorities for the garden – not an easy task when they weren't able to go out into the space! A decision was made to take the children to visit an organic garden nearby at Yalding and observe them in action. This visit was a resounding success and gave the project team very clear messages about children's perspectives. Children liked to run, balance and jump; they liked to be with their friends; they liked to have hideaways; they were interested in making sounds, sharing new experiences, digging in earth and planting. The children's interests were then incorporated into the plans for the garden and the project team realised that the way forward did not have to involve costly pieces of equipment. Their observations of children outdoors had helped them to recognise that the children's play and learning experiences could be provided for through low-cost resources that were modifiable according to their current interests.

Early years staff working with babies and children under two years old had a similar challenge. How were they to gather the perspectives of these very young children, many of whom had only limited verbal skills and not all of whom were mobile? In Glebe House Day Nursery staff working in the baby room built up a detailed picture of each child's perspective using a range of approaches (see Case study 2.5). Mary Sheridan Pre-school provides for children with special educational needs. The staff there used very similar techniques to give the children in their setting a 'voice' in the consultation process.

Recommended reading for further information: National Children's Bureau leaflets in the series Listening as a Way of Life: 'Listening to babies' by Diane Rich and 'Listening to young disabled children' by Mary Dickins.

Case study 2.5: Gathering views of babies and children under two years old
Glebe House Day Nursery

The babies and toddlers at Glebe House Day Nursery share use of the large garden with older children. They also have direct access from the Baby Room to a secluded balcony area for outdoor play. However, the space is undeveloped and underused so staff were keen to rectify this situation as part of their outdoor developments.

Below is a summary of the range of approaches used by staff to give even the very youngest children a 'voice' in the consultation process.

'Tuning in' to very young children

Key staff working directly with babies and toddlers were already naturally 'tuning in' to their interests and needs and through this daily interaction they identified several significant issues. The children were particularly interested in posting and retrieving objects from containers and boxes. They also liked pulling themselves up to standing position and 'cruising' round fixed objects.

Talking to parents

The Nursery staff in the Baby Room had a good rapport with parents, so it was easy to find out about children's outdoor activities and experiences elsewhere, for example in the local park or in the garden at home. Parents commented that children liked equipment that included opportunities to experience motion, such as rocking, rolling and see-sawing.

Observations

The Nursery implements an observation and assessment system that tracks children's progress towards developmental milestones. This record is used to help key workers plan further experiences that support the learning needs of individual children in their care. So each key worker contributed useful information to the consultation process.

The babies and toddlers at Glebe House Day Nursery were given a 'voice' by staff through a process that gathered information about their interests, preferences and concerns from as many sources as possible. Staff took time to really 'listen' and interpret these messages before focusing on developing their plans for outdoors. Inspiration from *Early Years Outdoors* and early years magazines provided staff with a useful focus for further discussion at team meetings and assisted them in implementing the next stage of their outdoor project.

Children can also participate in surveys of the outdoor area. Encourage them to identify hazards, find the shady or sunny areas, or record where water collects after rain. Consider providing disposable cameras for a photographic survey resulting in a display showing children's most and least favourite areas of the outdoor space. St John's Primary School and Pre-school used specific props to provide a focus for children's thoughts during the survey and make the activity more meaningful. (See Case study 2.6.)

Case study 2.6: Involving children in surveying the space
St John's Pre-school and Primary School

Children in the Pre-school and in the Reception class have adjoining classrooms and share use of the outdoor area. As part of the initial stages of their project, the staff were keen to involve children in surveying the space. A session was planned that involved children in both the Pre-school and the Reception class. The purpose of the activity was to explore with children how they viewed the existing space and to identify how it could be improved upon.

Using information gathered from earlier conversations with children about outdoors, staff decided to concentrate the session on identifying *places to dig, places to paint, places to hide, and places to run*. Simple props were made available to provide a focus for children's thinking, i.e. trowels, paintbrushes, cuddly toys and trainers. Children worked in small groups with an adult to discuss and identify the best options for these experiences. The information was then recorded using symbols on a plan of the outdoor space.

The staff found that the session revealed some interesting information, for example, all the children except one showed a clear preference for painting on vertical spaces, such as walls, windows and doors. Staff had to then evaluate whether this preference had arisen because of the existing lack of horizontal places for painting, or because children valued the extra opportunities that the outdoor environment provided for using vertical spaces. Taking the time to reflect on the observations made and the information gathered is vital to ensure that the project moves forward in the right direction.

A basket of props to provide a focus for children's thinking

The 'Getting started' prompt sheets at the end of this chapter provide further information and ideas for involving children in the early stages of developing outdoors.

Involving others

It is essential to seek out the opinions of other people. Include those people directly involved in the setting, such as parents, management, grounds maintenance staff. Also, consider the views of other users of the outdoor environment, for example parent and toddler groups, after-school clubs, youth clubs. The project team at MCNA Pre-school realised it is important not to overlook issues that may be of particular significance to other users. Conflict between user groups will arise if future changes have not taken account of everyone's needs. (See Case studies 2.7 and 2.8.)

Case study 2.7: Involving others in the development of the outdoor space MCNA Pre-school, Margate

The MCNA Pre-school is a community group that shares its accommodation and outdoor environment with other user groups in the neighbourhood. Consequently, it was vital that everyone was consulted about the plans for developing the outdoors, to ensure that any potential conflict could be resolved during the project design stage. Once the plans for the garden had been developed, staff shared their ideas with representatives from other user groups within the building. This revealed a significant problem with the planned layout; the proposed position of the sandpit was going to impact on the space used by children at the after-school club for their football games. However, the ensuing discussions between the pre-school and the after-school club led to a mutually agreeable compromise option and the design plans were adjusted to reflect the new position.

Case study 2.8: Gathering the views and perspectives of all users of the space Bedgebury Junior School

The space used by the nursery children was also used by older children, during break-time and lunchtime. Therefore it was vital that any development plans also took account of older children's existing use and their ideas and perspectives. As part of the consultation process children in Years 1 and 2 were asked to share their views through photographs, drawings and conversations. This information was then fed back to the early years staff involved in planning the developments outdoors.

For some settings the initial involvement and agreement of others is an absolute priority. St Martin's Pre-school in Folkestone uses a community centre adjacent to a playing field and car park. They needed the landowners to give permission for them to use and develop an area of the site before they could proceed with their plans. (See Case study 2.9.)

The staff at Saplings @ The Sports Centre had ongoing difficulties in securing their perimeter fencing before further developments could take place. Pupils at the adjacent secondary school kept damaging it in their efforts to retrieve their footballs. Providing a designated access gate for them solved the problem overnight!

Case study 2.9: Getting permission to use and develop an outdoor space
St Martin's Pre-school, Folkestone

Children at St Martin's Pre-school were already making some good use of the car park and adjoining field. However, staff were keen to fence and develop a plot of land outside the community centre for the pre-school's sole use, in order to enrich the outdoor curriculum and reduce the amount of time spent on monitoring children's movements and safety on the large playing field.

Initial enquiries revealed that the land was owned by the Armed Forces, managed by the community centre committee, and used by several groups including the local primary school. The supervisor at

St Martin's Pre-school recognised that for the pre-school to have any chance of achieving their aim they would have to put a very good case to several organisations.

The pre-school spent time carefully preparing their case; they used cones to map out the area under discussion and took photographs for their presentation. They put forward a clear proposal setting out why they needed the space, what they would use it for, how it would be maintained, and how the impact on other user groups would be kept to a minimum. Negotiations are still under way, however the staff at St Martin's Pre-school are hopeful that agreement will be reached shortly.

St Martin's Pre-School is keen to fence a plot of land

Prompt sheet 2.1

Involving children in 'Getting started'

Surveying the existing space: Tours (see Clark and Moss 2005: 37–9)

When to use this activity

Useful technique for

* active children who like to be on the move

* identifying favourite spaces in existing environments

* surveying existing features in the environment

* identifying features, items or activities of importance to the child.

Use this activity to build up detailed information about what children currently like to do outdoors.

Preparation and resources

Offer children a variety of methods for recording their views during the tour. Options could include

* cameras

* clipboards, pencils and paper

* audio or video tape recorders

* dictaphone.

Gathering the information

Individual children take an adult on a tour of the outdoor space. They can be given control of the route of the tour and how their preferences are recorded during the tour, and how they will be documented later.

Ask open questions, such as 'What happens in this part of the garden?'

Making sense of the information

Invite children to share their thoughts with other children or staff. Looking at the photographs, drawings or recordings will promote further discussion about the space and ensure that staff draw an accurate conclusion about children's views.

Issues to consider

Keep an open mind and try not to make assumptions about the information children provide. For example, for some children the importance of particular areas of the garden is strongly linked to whether or not it is associated with social interaction with friends rather than to the equipment that is sited there.

Prompt sheet 2.2

Involving children in 'Getting started'

Using prop sacks and treasure baskets

When to use this activity

Useful technique for

* identifying children's current perspectives and use of their environment

* helping very young children to focus on the process and purpose of the consultation

* involving active children who like to be on the move.

Preparation

Gather together a set of resources that will act as a focus for the consultation. Present these items to children in a drawstring sack or a basket. Use equipment that children will easily relate to, objects that they will understand the purpose of, and items for which children will be able to identify a use and context, such as:

picture book	seeds
trowel	watering can
doll	ball
car	blanket
sunglasses	wellington boots
windmill	paintbrush.

Each item is used to gather children's perspectives on a different aspect/feature of the outdoor space.

Gathering the information

An individual child, or a pair of children, works outdoors with an adult. They choose an item from the sack or basket, and then find the best place in the garden for the associated experience. For example, a child choosing the book from the basket would show the adult the best place for reading a story outdoors. Similarly, the child choosing sunglasses, a windmill, or wellington boots would find the sunniest, windiest or muddiest spot outdoors.

Making sense of the information

It is important to record the information children provide to allow it to form part of the emerging picture of the way the garden is currently used. A plan of the space is useful. Adults can note where children engage in different types of activities and their views on environmental features, such as sun and wind. Children can also be involved in recording information. Display photographs of the outdoor space and encourage children to stick a symbol or drawing next to the photo that shows the relevant part of the garden.

Issues to consider

Be aware that this may show up unexpected gaps in the existing outdoor provision; for example, if children feel that there is no suitable spot for story-telling. Ensure that any perceived gaps are addressed in the planned developments.

This activity can also be used in the thinking and planning stage with small world toys to identify where proposed new features could be sited. (See 'Thinking and planning' Prompt sheet 3.1.)

Prompt sheet 2.3

Involving children in 'Getting started'

Surveying the space: tours with an intermediary, such as a puppet or soft toy

When to use this activity

Useful technique for

* surveying existing features

* gathering children's perspectives on the existing provision

* identifying future priorities

* identifying favourite and important places

* children under three years old

* children with limited or undeveloped communication skills.

Use this activity to build up detailed information about what children currently like to do outdoors. The use of an intermediary, such as a named puppet or soft toy, can provide a focus for the survey with very young children. It is also a useful technique if the adult conducting the survey is not well known to the children; they may be reluctant to share their thoughts with an unfamiliar adult but will be happy to talk to the toy. Alternatively, very young children with a limited vocabulary or those with communication difficulties can use the soft toy to show an adult what happens in different parts of the garden (see Clark and Moss 2005: 102).

Preparation and resources

Introduce the puppet or toy, or use one that is already known to the children. It is easier if the puppet has a name for children and adults to refer to it by, for example 'Bertie'.

Consider taking photographs as a record of the survey findings and a catalyst for further discussions among staff and children.

Offer children some options for recording the survey findings, for example through drawings, photographs, or tape recordings.

Gathering the information

Individual children take 'Bertie' and an adult on a tour of the outdoor space. Either allow children to choose the route of the tour or ask them to show 'Bertie' where particular experiences take place.

Ask open questions, such as 'Can you show/tell Bertie what happens in this part of the garden?' or 'If Bertie wanted to hide in the garden where would he go?'

Making sense of the information

Invite the children involved in the tour to share their thoughts with other children or staff. Create a book using photographs or children's drawings to promote further discussion about the space. Create a display using Bertie and captioned photographs that identify what children think he could do in each part of the garden

Issues to consider

Keep an open mind; children's perspectives on the best place for Bertie to go for particular experiences may differ from the adult view. Also, the use of an intermediary can enable children to open up about more sensitive issues, such as why they have strong preferences for, or an aversion to, particular parts of the garden. These insights will need careful consideration by adults involved in planning the future development of the space.

Prompt sheet 2.4

Involving children in 'Getting started'

Interviews

When to use this activity

Useful technique for

* focusing in on children's perceptions of their everyday experiences

* gathering responses about a pre-prepared set of questions

* children who are able to verbalise their thoughts.

Preparation and resources

Work out in advance the questions that will be asked of children. Remember to phrase questions to encourage children to give a full response rather than just 'Yes' or 'No'. You may wish to include or adapt the following example questions:

What is the best thing about outdoors?

Can you think of anything about outdoors that you don't like?

Can you think of anything you would like to do outdoors that would make it a better place than it is now?

Is there anything you want to do outdoors that you are not allowed to do?

Provide a tape recorder to record children's responses.
(See Clark and Moss 2005: 45–51 for a detailed account of this technique in action.)

Gathering the information

Children participate in a short 'interview' or prepared questions and an adult records their responses. Children should be able to choose the place where the interview takes place. Some may prefer to participate outdoors while others might prefer a familiar spot indoors.

Making sense of the information

Listen to the children's taped responses and note any emerging patterns in their answers. Are there places or features outdoors that are particularly popular or unpopular? What experiences or features have children identified as possible improvements to their outdoor space? Have the interviews highlighted any other matters of importance or concern to children that need to be considered as part of the development plans for outdoors?

Issues to consider

Children may be comfortable being interviewed alone or they may prefer to participate with a friend. Some children will revel in the attention, however not all children will be comfortable with a lengthy session. It is therefore important that children are able to end the interview if they choose to.

Prompt sheet 2.5

Involving children in 'Getting started'

Finding out how children feel about the outdoor environment: happy tokens

When to use this activity

Useful technique for

* active children who like to be on the move

* identifying children's preferences in existing environments

* surveying opinions about existing features in the environment

* identifying features, items or activities of importance to the child.

Preparation and resources

Gather together several containers and some tokens. The tokens can be anything that is in plentiful supply, for example bricks, beads, buttons. However, take care that the size of the token does not represent a choking hazard to very young children.

Label the containers with a happy or sad face and a note of where they are to be sited. Place them in pairs around the outdoor area in key spots, for example by existing features, such as the climbing frame or the sandpit.

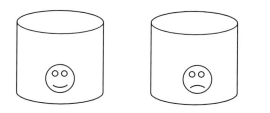

Gathering the information

Encourage children who visit each area to collect a token and drop it into the pot with the face that represents how they feel about the feature or space.

Making sense of the information

By counting the number of tokens in each pot it will be easy to establish preferences for particular areas of the garden. Children can help to count and collate the information onto a summary sheet.

Issues to consider

Some children may not have a strong preference for a particular area. Therefore it may be appropriate to introduce a third pot labelled with a neutral expression to allow these children to express their viewpoint.

It is possible to determine preferences linked to gender or age by giving children preordained tokens; for example, by using a particular colour or shape of token for boys/girls, or for children under/over three years old. This will provide further useful details that can be used to inform future plans.

Prompt sheet 2.6

Involving children in 'Getting started'

Finding out how children feel about the outdoor environment: cheer rating

When to use this activity

Useful technique for

* active children who like to be on the move

* identifying children's preferences in existing environments

* surveying opinions about existing features in the environment

* identifying features, items or activities of importance to the child.

Preparation and resources

This activity needs little preparation or resources. It is a very useful preliminary activity that can be used to get children used to the process of giving an opinion on aspects of their outdoor environment. Children express their preferences and levels of enthusiasm for different parts of the garden by cheering in each area. A tape recorder is a useful way to record children's responses.

Gathering the information

Having explained the activity to the children, visit each part of the garden with a small group and encourage them to cheer – loudly or quietly according to how they feel about the space. Consider using a tape recorder to document children's responses. Remember to mention on tape where each cheer takes place to help make sense of the recording afterwards.

Making sense of the information

It will be possible to form a general view about how children feel, through their cheer responses. This may confirm the view of adults in the setting or may offer new perspectives.

Issues to consider

This activity does not reveal accurate measurable information; however, it is fun and it will provide a broad overview about how children feel.

Thinking and planning

Developing the ideas

This stage of the process focuses on finding ways to develop the use of outdoors as a stimulating learning environment that is fully integrated with the use of indoors. The four Aspects of the *Birth to Three Matters Framework* include examples of experiences that very young children should have, both indoors and outdoors. Similarly, the *Curriculum Guidance for the Foundation Stage* includes a wealth of ideas for taking learning outdoors. All six areas of learning can be effectively promoted, from the earliest stepping stones through to the early learning goals at the end of Reception year. The information about children's current experiences, gathered through surveys and discussions, provides a good starting point for identifying gaps in the existing outdoor curriculum. These gaps may relate to one aspect of children's development, for example sound-making opportunities, or it may relate to a whole area of learning. (See Case study 3.1.)

Case study 3.1: Enriching the curriculum
Bell Wood Community Primary School,
Maidstone

Bell Wood Community Primary School is at the centre of a dilapidated estate of flats and houses in Maidstone. Many of the children attending the school have few outdoor experiences and little contact with the natural world. Foundation Stage staff had voiced a growing concern about children's under-achievement within the curriculum area promoting knowledge and understanding of the world. Children's aversion to insects and nature and their lack of respect for living plants and creatures were hampering their learning and progress. This concern was borne out by children's assessments at the end of the Foundation Stage. Analysis showed that children entered the school with very low levels of attainment in this area and, despite the best efforts of staff, at the end of the Foundation Stage children had not reached the early learning goals.

A survey among staff, parents and children

identified a plot of land in the school that was an underused eyesore and a decision was made to develop this area into a haven for wildlife. Staff recognised that development of the garden is a long-term project and they are aware that it will be some time before they know whether the initiative has achieved their key aim – to improve children's attitudes and experiences of the natural world and improve their attainment.

Children have contributed their ideas to a display about the garden and they have helped to select plants at the local garden centre. They have grown seeds, planted them out and watered them during the hot weather. The staff have reviewed the curriculum plans and embedded use of the new wildlife garden into the plans for children's learning to ensure that activities take place throughout the year. Children will be able to use the garden for observational and investigative work. Staff also intend that children will carry out many of the seasonal tasks necessary to tend and maintain the garden throughout the year.

Sunshine and Showers Nursery School: a storage area has been transformed

...into an outdoor art area!

However, curriculum development may not be the only focus of the project. Through the earlier stages of the consultation process the project team may have identified other problems that are hampering the development of the outdoor area; for example, limited or undeveloped space, lack of shade, concerns about vandalism or problems with storing equipment. The resolution of these wider issues is an equally important focus for the team and will be crucial to the success of the project. Both Happy Faces Pre-school and Sunshine and Showers Nursery School had to make significant changes to their grounds in order to improve children's curriculum experiences outdoors.

Starting to create a vision plan

A vision plan is a broad outline of the way the outdoor space is to be organised and improved, rather than a detailed plan of the precise developments. It defines the overall layout and structure and supports progress towards making the planned alterations, whether these are changes to the use, management or design of the outdoor area.

Before creating a vision plan it is useful to summarise the issues, problems or areas of conflict that have been identified and need to be resolved. Turn these issues into positive action statements and begin to prioritise them.

It is noticeable in Table 3.1 that some actions relate to management issues, for example staff development, and others involve physical changes, such as improving children's access to shade. Table 3.2 shows how MCNA Pre-school turned negative statements into positive action statements that identified what needed to happen next.

Having identified and prioritised the list of positive actions it is useful to circulate this information for comments before moving on to the next stage. Consider displaying the information for parents, sharing it at a staff meeting or management meeting, or publishing it in the next newsletter.

The next step towards the vision plan is the creation of a zone plan (see Figure 3.1). Zoning breaks up larger spaces into more manageable ones, and creates places where activities can be carried out harmoniously. When working out zones, it is better to concentrate on what children would like to be able to **do** in different areas rather than focusing on pieces of equipment to **have** in the space. This enables each solution to have a variety of responses. For example, rather than saying 'We want a sandpit here', settings were encouraged to consider how and where they could offer a variety of digging experiences. See pp. 16–18 for experiences that children should be able to DO outdoors. This is a useful starting point for further discussion among staff.

Table 3.1 Turning negative issues into positive action

Negative issues	Positive action
* 'The outdoor area is bleak and exposed'	* Create shelter and enclosures
* 'There is not enough shade'	* Improve shade facilities
* 'There are few opportunities for children to grow and care for plants'	* Develop an area for gardening
* 'Equipment keeps being stolen from the shed	* Improve the storage facilities
* 'The staff are not sure of their role outdoors'	* Address staff development needs
* 'Parents complain if the children get muddy'	* Address parental concerns about mud

Table 3.2 MCNA Pre-school: turning negative issues into positive action

Negative issue	Positive action	Next step
Lack of safety surface	Install safety surface	* Get two or three quotes for safety surface
No provision for children to explore sounds	Create sound area	* Identify place for sound-making * Get hold of unwanted saucepans etc.
No provision for children to draw outdoors	Develop mark-making opportunities, fixed and moveable	* Provide blackboards attached to shed * Supply clipboards and pencils
Insufficient surfaces/ pathways for bikes and wheeled toys	Review and improve provision of bikes and wheeled toys	* Identify minimum width needed to enable children to ride bikes and pass each other * Work out a scale plan for the cycle track and position of pebble roundabout * Visit local example of pebbles with children
No provision for children to care for plants/ observe seasonal changes in their environment	Develop planted area that changes with the seasons NB After-school club: consider implications for playing football	* Create raised flower bed in corner of garden – therefore minimal impact on football activities and plants given greater protection
No provision for sand play	Provide a sandpit NB consider sunken pit to ensure access by SEN child NB After-school club: consider implications for playing football	* Identify best size and position for new sandpit * Research manufacturers

It's important to consider how children move around the play space and provide areas that separate different kinds of experiences, as well as places for children to safely stop and consider what they wish to do next.

The purpose of the zone plan is to:

* identify and define the main areas in the outdoor space

* site activities and equipment in the best possible location (or zone)

* resolve any major physical site problems and conflicts.

In order to minimise the potential for conflict within the space, ensure that the layout of the area locates complementary zones adjacent to one another. Some settings have zoned their play areas into 'Active – Transition – Quiet'; others have used a 'Work – Rest – Play' division. Each setting's situation is different, so it is essential to involve everyone in this part of the project. See 'Thinking and planning' prompt sheets at the end of

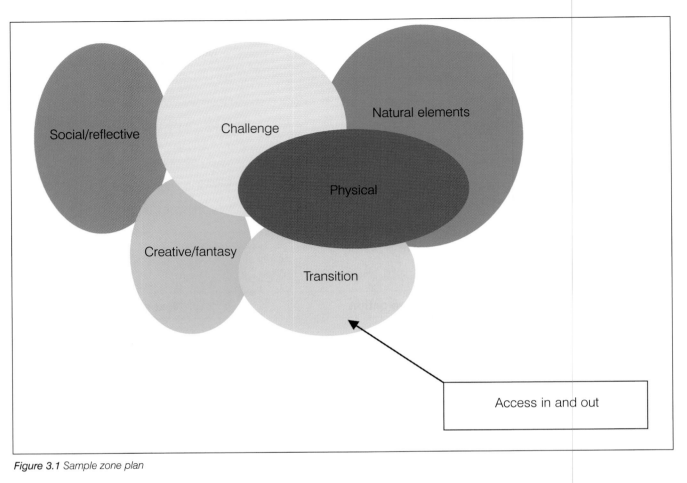

Figure 3.1 Sample zone plan

Source: LTL Developmental Site Visit Service

this chapter for specific ideas for involving children in this stage of the project. It may take several draft versions to reach the final zone plan that everyone is happy with.

Useful questions to ask:

What is the best possible location for a specific use?

Where else could it be sited?

What can we shift or change to reduce conflict or improve use?

Is the space large enough for its purpose?

Does its location conflict with any of the surrounding uses?

Does the space have two major uses which will affect its siting?

Does it need to be near the buildings?

How will its location affect its maintenance and management?

Does the orientation of the area affect it?

Once the different zones have been identified and mapped out on the plan, the next step is to find ways of identifying the zones in the actual space, so that staff and children can use each area appropriately and to its full potential. There are many ways of dividing up space – and they don't all involve physical barriers. In many early years settings, space is at a premium, therefore its organisation has to be flexible, to allow for any number of alternative uses. Consequently, it is important to consider ways of defining zones that will enhance the overall effectiveness of the space. For example:

* Mark out lines and patterns on the ground – especially good for containing the movement of children on wheelie toys.

* Use low hedging or fencing to separate a quiet area.

* Temporary zoning can be done using traffic cones, chalk markings or tables – or even milk and bread crates. Children can have fun deciding where each play zone will be on a daily or weekly basis, and turning zone dividers into dens and other play structures.

* A more permanent solution could be to build raised planting beds to divide areas. These also have the advantage of potentially providing greenery in the play area, and allowing children to grow their own plants, or to dig holes and generally get mucky!

* Knee rails (a low timber rail which children can also sit on) and bollards can both play a part in zoning spaces.

The project team will need to check the zone plan against the initial site survey information. Make sure that the zone plan takes account of pathways and access routes for vehicles and other users. Ensure that conflicts have been resolved and that where possible special places or important features have been retained or re-sited. Before taking the next step it is useful to make a final copy of the zoning plan and display it prominently for feedback and comments. At Victoria Road Primary School a three-dimensional model of the ideas for the playground was displayed in the school library to allow a wider audience to comment on the plans so far, while at Ditton Church Pre-school a more detailed plan was displayed and comments invited from parents (Figure 3.2).

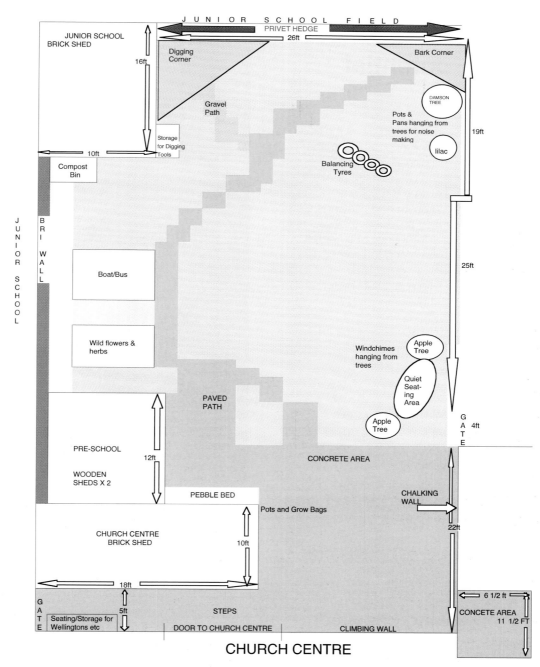

Figure 3.2 Ditton Church Pre-school's draft plan

Identifying potential solutions

This stage of the process identifies in detail the potential changes to the use, design or management of the space that are needed. This phase will need to be repeated for each issue in the different areas of the site and the changes may not just be through developing the space and its physical features. In Kent, settings also considered the resources they provided, their planning techniques, the amount and frequency of time that outdoors is available to children and the role and deployment of adults.

As part of the process of finding solutions for each issue it is necessary to identify:

* who needs to be consulted

* what action needs to be taken

* who will co-ordinate the action

* who needs to be contacted about implementation.

The settings had different needs, and the solutions to the problems they faced were wide-ranging and varied. However, it is possible to group some issues into broad categories, such as the following.

Management and organisational changes

These might include changes to the deployment and responsibilities of staff, improving children's access, and reorganisation of storage facilities.

Training/increasing knowledge

This may include courses for teaching or non-teaching staff as well as in-service training sessions that look at specific aspects of outdoor provision, for example mathematical development. It may incorporate visits to other settings or outdoor centres for inspiration and exchange of ideas. It may mean collecting and sharing information or materials that support teaching and learning outdoors.

Resources – acquisition or renovation

An audit of existing resources and site features may reveal some that are worn or neglected, as well as highlighting the gaps in current provision. It is important to identify any underlying problems. Why do resources need renewing or replacing? Is storage or vandalism a problem? If so, these issues need addressing before precious funds are spent replacing equipment.

Design solutions – making physical changes

This may include improving seating or shade facilities. It may include the removal of unwanted features, the development of a wildlife garden or the installation of an all-weather canopy.

Gathering everyone's viewpoints on the different options will be vital. Children can offer some very important perspectives on design solutions (see Case study 3.2). For ideas for involving children in identifying design solutions, see 'Thinking and planning' Prompt sheet 3.5.

All weather canopy at Sunshine and Showers Nursery School

Case study 3.2: Involving children in developing designs
Victoria Road Primary School, Ashford

Having carried out extensive consultations within the whole-school community, the issues were very clear. The children's main concerns focused on the following areas:

* seating

* ball recovery from the other side of fences and walls

* den-building facilities

* stepping stones.

The staff had identified their concerns about

* the barren environment

* the children's lack of opportunities to experience the natural world

* lack of opportunities for creative development.

The wider school community had been consulted and their perspectives were also taken into account and revealed the following information. The playground was also used

* by older children, therefore any new structures had to be suitable for all ages or removable at break time;

* by midday supervisors pushing trolleys between the kitchen and dining hall

* as an access route for occasional yet essential oil deliveries.

The next stage was to involve children in developing some solutions that would enrich the playground environment for the Foundation Stage pupils without compromising the requirements of other users of the space. The inspiration for the design session was loosely based around the 'Planning for Real' initiative. This concept has been used successfully to consult with urban communities about the regeneration of their neighbourhood. However, it was necessary to adapt the idea to suit younger participants, so small world toys were used initially to explore some of the design problems. Then, rather than using a small-scale model, staff and children went outside to develop and design solutions within the actual space.

Initially a 'Circle Time' session was used to introduce the idea of a 'Planning For real' activity. Small world dolls, construction toys and recyclable materials were used to represent and develop an imaginary playground. This small world activity focused on the ideas already identified as of concern to the children. Later the same day everyone went outside to explore and experiment with the space in the playground. Each group of six children had an adult supporting them. Each group were asked to develop one area of the playground and find a design solution to any problems they encountered. They were given access to a variety of materials to aid the design process, for example PE equipment, such as bases for ball games, hoops, quoits, skipping ropes and a parachute, as well as items of classroom furniture, plant pots and recyclable resources, such as cardboard boxes. The session proved to be a very creative experience, with children deeply involved in working through their ideas and finding solutions to the difficulties they faced. At the end of the session the groups shared their problems and solutions with everyone. Staff noted these comments and the children's ideas were incorporated into the final design plan for the playground. Afterwards the children returned to the classroom to record their thoughts and ideas through drawings and paintings.

Children at Victoria Road Primary School designing a new seating area. See Prompt Sheet 3.5 and p.56 for more information

Prompt sheet 3.1

Involving children in 'Thinking and planning'

Using models and plans

When to use this activity

Useful technique for

* deciding where new features should be in the space

* considering the impact of different layouts.

Preparation

Prepare a model or plan. This may be more meaningful to children if it is done in conjunction with them. Decide how to represent the planned features, for example small laminated images or symbolic objects.

Gathering the information

Children can position the representations of planned features in different places on the model or plan in response to questions such as

* 'Where would you like the quiet area/sandpit/ digging pit to be?'

Making sense of the information

Talk about the options with children as they participate. Consider capturing individual children's ideas through photographs for further review and discussion.

Issues to consider

Older children may be able to make sense of a two-dimensional plan of the space but younger children may find it easier to work with a three-dimensional model.

Consider using symbolic props with younger children or children who prefer to work directly in their outdoor space when thinking about these questions. (See 'Getting started', Prompt sheet 2.2.)

Prompt sheet 3.2

Involving children in 'Thinking and planning'

Developing ideas by visits to other developed outdoor environments

When to use this activity

Useful technique for

* observing children's use of equipment and environments

* widening children's experiences and awareness of potential solutions

* gathering children's opinions

* enabling children to make decisions based on a real experience

* involving parents.

Preparation

As with any other visit off-site, careful attention must be given to preparation. Settings should follow the appropriate procedures before embarking on an off-site visit; for example, gaining parental permission, ensuring adequate staffing, completing a pre-visit risk assessment.

Ensure that the setting or place to be visited includes the type of features that are under consideration.

Consider how children's reactions, comments or views will be recorded during the visit. Options could include video or tape recorder, camera or notes.

Gathering the information

Observe children during the visit and discuss their experiences with them. Talk to the adults and children in the visited setting to gather their views about specific pieces of equipment.

Making sense of the information

Afterwards, provide opportunities to discuss the visit further, for example by encouraging children to record their thoughts via drawings and paintings. If photos have been taken, consider creating a display and offering children the chance to vote on their favourite experience during the visit (see Prompt sheet 3.4).

Issues to consider

The settings or places visited will need to be chosen carefully to ensure that the experiences that children have are a feasible option for their own environment.

Children using unfamiliar equipment for the first time may react differently to the experience from children who are familiar with it.

Prompt sheet 3.3

Involving children in 'Thinking and planning'

Recording information through 'mapping' activities

When to use this activity

Useful technique for

* collating all the information gathered through earlier consultations with children, for example through tours of the space (see 'Getting started', Prompt sheet 2.1).

* providing a composite visual record of the places and spaces outdoors considered important by children

* sharing children's perspectives with a wider audience, for example other children, parents, staff or management.

Preparation

Provide a large piece of paper and copies of materials generated by individual children during the initial consultations, for example their photographs and drawings from tours. Gather together additional resources such as pencils, crayons, paper, glue-sticks.
(See Clark and Moss 2005: 39–43 for a detailed account of this technique in action.)

Gathering the information

Work with one or two children to make a 'map' of outdoors. Support the children to select the images and materials that they want to show on their map. Encourage them to add further information, for example by drawing or writing on the map. Offer to add captions of children's comments.

Making sense of the information

Ongoing conversations during the map-making activity will provide valuable insights into children's thoughts and priorities. The map-makers can be offered the opportunity to share their map with other children or staff. The finished maps can be displayed prominently to encourage further discussion.

Issues to consider

Some children may find it hard to relinquish 'their' photographs for a shared map-making activity. Consider providing each child with a set of their photographs to keep, and offer copies of all materials to be used for map-making.

Alison Clark working with children at Happy Faces Pre-school

Prompt sheet 3.4

Involving children in 'Thinking and planning'

Using photographs to identify priorities

When to use this activity

Useful technique for

* identifying and ranking children's preferences and priorities across a range of options, for example seating, sandpit, growing area

* identifying and ranking children's preferences for the options in relation to a specific feature, for example a raised/sunken/large/small sandpit

* involving children in development of the vision plan.

Preparation

On the basis of the information gathered from everyone, make up a set of photographs that show the options for development, for example a sandpit, a gardening area, seating, playhouse.

Or make up a set of photographs that show a variety of options for a specific feature, such as various types of seating.

Draw up a chart to record children's preferences and priorities.

Gathering the information

Show individual children two photographs at a time and ask them to decide which is the best/most important.

Record the favoured option on the chart and continue for all pairs.

Making sense of the information

Count the number of times an option has been favoured and place all the options in a rank order, for example:

Ranking different features		*Ranking the options for one feature*	
Sandpit	4	Large sandpit	4
Growing area	3	Sunken sandpit	3
Playhouse	2	Raised sandpit	2
Seating	1	Small sandpit	1

Issues to consider

Avoid overwhelming children with too many decisions. Make sure that the options shown to children are feasible and under real consideration.

Prompt sheet 3.5

Involving children in 'Thinking and planning'

Developing designs

When to use this activity

Useful technique for

* solving design problems

* overcoming potential conflicts in the layout of features or equipment

* checking the impact of different features in the space

* active children who prefer to work in a space rather than with representational materials

Preparation

Assemble a collection of objects and materials that can be used by children to symbolise a feature or to mark out an area; for example, carpet tiles, skipping ropes, lining paper, bamboo canes, blankets, hoops, cones, plastic bricks, cardboard boxes. Remember, anything can be used to represent anything!

Gathering the information

Work with small groups of children to achieve the aim of the session. For example, the purpose may be to decide the position and size of a new sandpit, or to work out a route around the garden for wheeled toys, or to consider the impact of allocating part of the garden to children under two years old, or to work out the design of seating. Encourage children to use the materials provided to work through the design issues and help them to think through and resolve any ensuing problems. For example, children may decide that potted plants growing along a fence will improve the look of the fence and stop balls rolling under it, but will the gate still open?

Making sense of the information

Use a camera to capture the stages of children's thinking and the different ideas and designs that are tried out before the final solution is found. Once developed, these photographs provide a valuable record of the session as well as providing useful material for displays or a book, to prompt further discussion. Page 56 shows children at Victoria Road Primary School designing their new seating area. A 3-D model that shows children's final designs is a very good way to reaffirm the ideas that have been developed and share them with a wider audience.

Issues to consider

Some children become despondent very quickly if their initial idea is found to have 'flaws'. Support children to see the session as a positive problem-solving process and encourage them to think of ways to adapt their ideas and try again.

Page 56 shows children at Victoria Road Primary School designing their new seating area.

Victoria Road Primary School, Ashford

See Case Study 3.2 for further information.

Children deciding on the design for their new seating area

The final design idea – a winding seat with plants (represented by the rope)

The new seating area

4 Making it happen

Developing an implementation plan

Once the vision plan has been produced, the use of each area has been decided upon and the potential solutions have been identified, the implementation or action plan needs to be developed. This sets out the steps and stages for turning the development plans for outdoors into a reality.

In preparing the implementation plan there are a number of issues to record:

* the specific elements of the project

* timescale and order of proceeding

* who will do the work

* whether specialist advice is needed

* how children will be involved

* types of materials required

* any technical and legal requirements

* contact details and quotations from suppliers and contractors

* costs

* funding sources

* completion target date.

The plan helps sort out and keep track of the tasks to be accomplished. It also provides a project record that may be a useful support to funding applications. (See Figures 4.1 and 4.2.)

Several settings successfully involved families, the local community and businesses in the implementation of their plans. By seeking donations and making good use of volunteer support precious funds can be preserved for services and materials that must be paid for.

Children at Glebe House Day Nursery helping to plant donated apple trees

Case study 4.1: Involving others to 'make it happen'
Bertie's Playgroup

Bertie's Playgroup uses a classroom at Ethelbert Road Infant School. They have sole use of a fenced area of the playground just outside the classroom. Staff and children make good use of their outdoor area but recognise that it could be improved. A clear vision plan was formed, based on their consultations with staff, parents and children. One of the emerging priorities for outdoors was improved storage that was accessible to children. The outdoor area was

surveyed to identify the best site for a new storage facility and it became apparent that a large raised flowerbed would need to be removed.

To keep costs to a minimum a decision was made to appeal for help in breaking up and removing the bed. A letter and notice to parents resulted in offers of labour and tools, staff also volunteered to help. The date was set, the skip was ordered, and one sunny Saturday morning the volunteers assembled at school to accomplish their task.

Several back-breaking hours later, the skip was full and the area was cleared and ready to be prepared for the shed base. The collection of the skip from the school playground on Monday was an unexpected highlight for the children, who were able to watch it being lifted and taken away.

Case study 4.2: Involving others to 'make it happen'
Highways at Hamstreet Kindergarten

This setting enlisted the help of families, the school and businesses in the community to implement their plans for the garden. They held a very successful 'Groundforce Day' and invited children and parents to come and help with a variety of tasks, such as fencing, painting, path laying and weaving. The provision of soup and rolls gave everyone a break at lunchtime and the energy to carry on afterwards.

The kindergarten also participated in an activity week organised in conjunction with the adjoining school. During the week children and staff worked hard to transform their recently erected pergola into a spectacular sensory experience

The staff also had significant success in attracting donations and gifts from businesses in their local

community. The local golf clubs gave unwanted balls, the local garden centre donated some 'end-of-line' pots and planters. The supervisor attributes their success to having an upfront attitude towards asking people and being able to give potential donors a clear message about the importance of

what they were trying to achieve and the significant benefit to children from the donations.

Case study 4.3: Involvement and support from business Bell Wood Community Primary School

Learning through Landscapes, in partnership with electricity supplier EDF Energy, runs an annual award scheme to recognise and reward good practice outdoors in school grounds. EDF Energy also offers their employees the opportunity to take part in a 'Team Challenge Day'. Each Challenge Team volunteers their labour for a day, and they have a small budget to provide some materials.

Bell Wood Community Primary School were an ideal candidate for a Team Challenge. The school were working hard to make their plans to turn land that was an underused eyesore into a haven for wildlife. The work had begun but progress was slow and other priorities within the school were taking precedence. Consequently, key personnel involved in the project were becoming anxious at the lack of momentum. The EDF Energy team took up the challenge to finish the fencing, help with planting the wildlife garden, and replant the flowerbed at the school entrance. The day was a great success and the school were thrilled with the progress that had been made in such a short time. It gave staff and children renewed impetus and enthusiasm to finish the wildlife garden and start using it.

The rest of this chapter features a selection of illustrative case studies that explore how some of the most common issues faced by early years practitioners were overcome through the project in Kent. The Prompt sheets at the end of the chapter give details of some of the ways that children were involved in 'making it happen' in their outdoor space.

The imagination and creativity shown by practitioners and project teams in seeking and identifying solutions is an inspiration and shows that, with determination, even the most challenging problems can be significantly reduced, or completely overcome.

Finding solutions to management and organisational issues

Case study 4.4: Carrying out a risk assessment before introducing free-flow access to outdoors Sunshine and Showers Nursery, St Mary's Bay

The staff at Sunshine and Showers Nursery were keen to introduce free-flow access to outdoors and planned to provide an environment that offered children risk and challenge. However, they recognised that a free-flow system would have implications for staffing levels both indoors and outdoors and therefore needed to be carefully planned and implemented to ensure that levels of safety were maintained. As part of their preparations for introducing the new system they carried out a risk assessment on their outdoor space. The staff

recognised that parents would each have a unique and valuable perspective on the potential risks for their own child so they invited parents to be involved in the initial assessment.

After an information session to outline the nursery's plans for developing the outdoor space, parents were given an opportunity to tour the garden with staff and identify any areas or features that they felt would give rise to an unacceptable risk for their child. The collaborative session with parents was constructive and purposeful, and parental worries were noted. Further meetings were held to allow staff to voice their concerns. The Accident Record Book provided another source of information for analysis by staff. After all the information had been gathered and reviewed, the plans for the garden progressed smoothly and free-flow access was introduced with full parental support. The staff continue to review their procedures, consult with parents and analyse the Accident Book to ensure that children benefit from the natural challenges that the garden offers, such as climbing in the bushes, while being protected from unacceptable levels of risk.

See Bibliography for details of a publication that promotes the importance of risk and challenge in young children's lives, *Too Safe for Their Own Good*, by Jennie Lindon.

Case study 4.5: Introducing free-flow access to outdoors
Happy Faces Pre-school, Tonbridge

The pre-school children had direct access to an enclosed outdoor space yet were only able to use it at prescribed times during the day. As the project progressed staff recognised the need to increase children's opportunities to be outdoors. However, they had to overcome several organisational issues in order to implement a new system that allowed children to flow freely between the indoor and outdoor environments. Below is a summary of the issues and concerns debated by staff. The solutions that they found indicate that a positive and creative problem-solving attitude works wonders, and has a positive impact on the provision being made both indoors and outdoors.

Issue	Suggestion	Advantages	Concerns	Solutions	Impact
Access route	Use the fire door at the rear of one classroom	Direct route	Classroom becoming cold as children entered and left	Re-organise use of space in hallway and use double doors next to cloakroom area	Improved access direct from hall and cloakroom area. Classroom remains warm
Children's management of coats and wellies	Encourage children towards independence	Children develop useful skills. Not dependent on adult help	Children not properly protected from extreme weather conditions. Cloakroom area untidy	Trial period introduced to see how the system would work	Most children quickly learnt to manage their outdoor clothes themselves. Staff reassured. Minimal support given to a few children that needed it
Staff deployment and maintaining ratios	Staff to be deployed to work in designated areas, including outdoors	Staff clear about roles and responsibilities. Children have adult support outdoors	Ratios not maintained since staff not always responding to the variations in numbers as children flow between indoors and outdoors	Discussion among staff team to ensure that all felt confident and able to use their initiative and redeploy themselves indoors/outdoors should the need arise	Staff more confident and move freely between indoors and outdoors as necessary. Staff able to give better support to children as their play develops

Case study 4.6: Overcoming staff reservations about introducing free-flow access to outdoors
Highways at Hamstreet Kindergarten

Very early on in the Space to Grow project the staff at Highways at Hamstreet Kindergarten were already supporting children to make good use of outdoors for a significant part of both the morning and afternoon sessions. They had overcome all initial hurdles, such as identifying an independent access route, ensuring that the garden was securely fenced, the development of good resources, the provision of suitable clothing and wellies, and engaging the support of parents. However, puzzlingly, they had not yet taken the final step of introducing 'free-flow' access.

Discussion with the supervisor revealed a deep-rooted anxiety about maintaining children's safety outdoors in the garden under a free-flow system.

Task	Who will lead?	Timescales	Useful contacts	Who will carry out the work?	How will children be involved?	Materials needed	Technical or legal issues	Costs	Funding source	Completion target date

Remember to keep a record of all the consultation and activity work you have completed with the children, as this can often provide important information for funders when applying for financial support with a project.

Figure 4.1 Example of an implementation plan

Learning through LANDSCAPES

Barrier to improving outdoor play	Action	Involvement of Children	Responsibility	Resources	Cost	Timescale	Monitoring progress – how and who	Evaluating success
Lack of safety surface	Get two or three quotes for safety surface / Install safety surface		Sheila	Supplied by contractor	To be confirmed	End of March	Sheila to send Gail quotes	Safety surface down by end of April
No provision for children to explore sounds	Get hold of unwanted saucepans etc. / Create sound area – on railings	Decorate saucepans	Sheila to co-ordinate efforts of staff team/ parents etc.	Time – hunting at jumble sales and car boot sales etc.	£20?	End of March	Sheila to keep Gail informed / Saucepans in situ by end of March / Send Gail photos	Children able to explore sounds outside
No provision for children to draw outdoors	Provide blackboards attached to shed	Can help identify position on shed – right height	Staff team	Time – preparing and painting boards	£30?	End of March	Sheila to keep Gail informed / Blackboards in situ by end of March / Send Gail photos	Children able to draw outside
Lack of surface for bikes and wheeled toys	Identify minimum width needed to enable children to ride bikes and pass each other / Work out a scale plan for the cycle track and position of pebble roundabout / Visit local example of pebbles with children	Children to paint pebbles	Sheila: Co-ordinate visit with Mark / Staff to plan for painting sessions with children	Paving slabs / Cement / Volunteer help?	To be confirmed Send Gail two or three estimates re the cost of extending the cycle track	End of April	Sheila to keep Gail informed / Let Gail know dates of visit re pebbles / Send Gail a scale drawing of proposed cycle track / Take photos of the children painting their pebble	Cycle track and pebble round about in place by end of April / Children using track after Easter holidays
No provision for children to care for plants/ observe seasonal changes in their environment	Develop raised flower bed	Fill bed with earth	Sheila with help from Paul Boyce (the garden gate)	Planting seeds and plants	To be confirmed Send Gail two or three estimates re the cost	End of March ? in time for planting	Sheila to keep Gail informed of progress / Take photos	Children able to plant after Easter holidays
No provision for sand play	Provide a sandpit – sunken to ensure access by SEN child / Identify best size and position for new sandpit	Discuss and trial position using temporary sandpit	Sheila		To be confirmed Send Gail two or three estimates	By beginning of Summer term	Sheila to keep Gail informed of progress / Take photos	Children using sandpit by May half term

Figure 4.2 Draft Action Plan MCMA Pre-school

Interestingly, this stance was at odds with her general attitude towards outdoor play, which was positive and acknowledged the importance of children experiencing risk and challenge in their lives. Further probing revealed that her concern was very specific: how to keep children safe when the garden was adjacent to a busy road with only a single gate in-between. This worry was exacerbated by other adults using the gate to enter the kindergarten at unspecified times.

The solution was a combination of common sense and discussion among staff and with parents, combined with the introduction of a system of sensible precautions to minimise the risk of a child inadvertently slipping through the gate. To her credit the supervisor overcame her own high level of anxiety in order to lead the staff towards resolving this issue. In a subsequent review all staff recognised that the introduction of a free-flow system had been a resounding success.

Case study 4.7: Free-flow access – keeping children safe in summer
Bright Beginnings Day Nursery, Dartford

The staff and children moved into their brand-new building in September 2003. The beginning of the Space to Grow project coincided with this move and provided a catalyst for developing the outdoor environment from the remains of a building site into a stimulating place for play and learning. An initial decision was made to focus on familiarising children with the indoor environment for the first few months, and to begin consultations about the development of outdoors in the spring term.

The plans for outdoors progressed well and by the summer term staff and children were enjoying periods of free-flow access to outdoors throughout the day. However, the summer months revealed a problem – a lack of shade over much of the play area. This naturally gave rise to discussions about the importance of keeping children safe in the sun and staff identified the need to devise a system whereby children were protected without losing their free access to outdoors.

First, parents were requested to supply sun cream and ensure their child was protected on arrival at

nursery. Permission was also sought from parents to allow staff to reapply sun cream as necessary. The next stage involved stationing a member of staff under the large covered veranda area just outside the exit doors, to ensure that the first time each child chose to go outside sun cream was applied and a note made of the time. The combination of sun cream, sun hats and covering up, coupled with an emphasis on activities under the veranda on particularly hot days, kept children safe and protected and enabled them to continue to benefit from their outdoor area.

Case study 4.8: Introducing free-flow access in a Reception class
Mongeham Primary School, Mongeham

The two Reception classes at Mongeham Primary School shared use of an enclosed outdoor area and staff valued the opportunities that outdoor play offers. However, they recognised the need for a system for monitoring and managing children's use of the space.

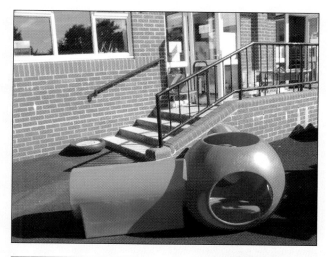

The indoor classroom was already organised to allow children to select the activities they wished to engage in, through a 'peg and picture' system. This system gave children choice and independence but let staff predetermine the number of children at any one activity. Children quickly learnt that if there was no space for their peg they would need to find an alternative. Initially this system was extended to give children an opportunity to choose 'outdoor toys' by placing their peg on the corresponding picture and going outside. Once this routine had been successfully established staff refined it further by providing pictures of different outdoor resources and experiences. This acted as a catalyst for children's play and also ensured that the numbers of children using specific pieces of equipment did not constitute a safety hazard.

By putting in place effective systems that gave children independence in both the indoor and outdoor environments staff were relieved of patrolling and head-counting duties and were able to focus on supporting children's play and learning.

Case study 4.9: Improving children's access to outdoors
Saplings @ The Sports Centre, Tunbridge Wells

Saplings @ The Sports Centre is accommodated in an upstairs room within the sports centre. The nursery management have negotiated use of a piece of land behind the centre to enable children and staff to access outdoors. However, the route to this outdoor area is via stairs, corridors, doors and locked gates, so allowing children independent access is not a feasible option. Discussion with staff revealed further issues to be overcome: ensuring the security of equipment and the practicalities of resourcing and setting up an outdoor area so far away from the indoor environment.

Despite these difficulties the day nursery staff were enthusiastic about outdoors. They were eager to find a way of developing the area and giving children a significant amount of time in it. Their determination and persistence paid off and a practical solution was eventually identified – the creation of an 'outdoor classroom'. The project award enabled the day nursery to purchase a large secure storage shed with wide doors. The shed was organised and equipped to allow children to independently access and return the resources they needed for their play.

This option addressed all the identified issues: it reduced concerns about security, it minimised the amount of 'setting up' needed, and it allowed resources and equipment to be stored permanently within the outdoor area, rather than being

transported there on a daily basis by staff. The staff are very pleased with the progress that has been made and the creation of an 'outdoor classroom' has provided a good starting point for further development and use of the space.

Case study 4.10: Overcoming a lack of space Pipsqueaks Day Nursery, Isle of Sheppey

Pipsqueaks Day Nursery is a privately owned and recently established day nursery on the Isle of Sheppey. The day nursery has very limited outdoor space on-site, little more than an alley. The staff recognise the importance of children accessing outdoors and regularly take the children to a local memorial park. The focus of the developments at Pipsqueaks Day Nursery has been to enrich children's learning experiences in the local public spaces and to improve the outdoor learning on-site. Having observed what children liked to do both indoors and at the local park, the staff used this

information to inform their development plans. The two key issues were to find ways to make best use of the limited space on-site and to improve children's play and learning experiences in the park.

An initial review of the access in and out of the nursery indicated that, with some minor adjustments, children could be given free-flow access to the alley from the rear of the building. This immediately increased the amount of time that they could spend outside and took pressure off the space since not all children accessed it simultaneously. Staff have also made imaginative use of the vertical wall space to maximise children's experiences and opportunities for learning. For example, oven racks and crepe paper offer children chances to weave and develop co-ordination of hand and eye movements. Using brushes to 'paint' different surfaces with water provides children with opportunities to observe changes to materials; for example, as the wall-mounted slate tiles turn from being dull grey to shiny black. A shelf unit against one wall is used to store small boxes of equipment for children to access and choose from during the session. Netting and old CDs suspended above children's heads create extra interest without using up valuable floor space.

To improve the provision being made in the park, staff have collected a range of resources that are multi-functional and lightweight. For example, younger children use a clothes airer and some lengths of material to make dens, but older children also use the airer with pegs for mathematical sorting opportunities. Balls and hoops support physical development. Washing-up bowls are used as stepping stones and for imaginative games. Each day children are involved in choosing what is transported on a trolley to the park. The box of musical instruments is a popular choice, and children also like re-enacting favourite stories, such as 'We're Going on a Bear Hunt'.

Case study 4.11: Sharing outdoor space
St John's Primary School and Pre-school

The Reception children at St John's Primary School share their outdoor space with the committee-run pre-school in the adjoining classroom. The two staff teams have worked together to identify their joint and individual priorities for developing the space. There have been many issues to resolve and hurdles to overcome and some are still under discussion. The table below highlights some of the key dilemmas faced by the staff, as well as some of the potential solutions.

Issue	Staff concerns	Potential solutions	Advantages
Responsibility for setting up and tidying away the outdoor area	For organisational reasons, specific tasks will be carried out by one team rather than shared by both	Ensure that equipment is stored in low-level labelled units	Children can select and return equipment themselves No need for either staff team to 'set up' or tidy away outdoor area
Deployment of staff	Both staff teams have several areas to supervise, both indoors and outdoors Because each team works under different management systems and has to conform to different regulations it is not possible to share responsibility for staffing outdoors	Consider staff deployment as separate teams, to allow each team to find own solutions. Then look at the two solutions together to see how they would work in tandem outdoors	Enables each staff team to meet their different statutory regulations regarding ratios

Issue	Staff concerns	Potential solutions	Advantages
Use of equipment and resources by different age groups (two–five years)	The two staff teams work with children who may have up to a three-year difference in age Not all equipment is suitable for children at either end of this age spectrum	Jointly evaluate all existing equipment and consider its suitability for the full age range Consider the full age range of children when adding new equipment to the area Identify the purpose of different pieces of equipment and consider how older/younger children might use them Label and organise storage to ensure that specific pieces of equipment that are really only appropriate for under-threes or over-fives are only accessible to these children Discuss storage and organisation with children and develop a shared and understood system for the use of different items, for example: * items in the blue cupboard are only to be used by two-year-olds * items in the red cupboard must be used with an adult	Most equipment will be suitable for all children – although they may well use it in different ways Both staff teams and all children have been involved in developing and implementing the system, therefore the system is more likely to be adhered to by all. A small range of specific items of equipment is protected from inappropriate use by older/younger children
Long-term maintenance of the area and seasonal replacement of resources, for example sand, seeds	How to share out the cost and responsibility for the replacement and replenishment of outdoor items	Review the existing system: * Discuss the existing roles and responsibilities among both staff teams, senior management and grounds maintenance staff * Identify current levels of expenditure on maintaining the outdoor space * Identify which budgets are currently being used Consider creating a shared budget that is contributed to by both the pre-school and the primary school Use this fund to cover ongoing expenditure and maintenance costs Agree any changes to the roles and responsibilities of existing grounds maintenance staff	The creation of a shared budget will ensure that future expenditure on the garden can be financed and will provide for the longer-term maintenance of the shared space

Case study 4.12: Developing outdoor provision despite an uncertain future
Mary Sheridan Pre-school, Canterbury

Mary Sheridan Pre-school is situated on premises with a large garden and it provides for children with special educational needs. When the pre-school originally joined the project the aim was to develop the large garden. However, it became apparent that the pre-school's future in their current premises was uncertain, and that at some point relocation to a different building was very likely.

Having established children's enthusiasms and interests, the pre-school staff reviewed their original plans and after some discussion the new plans focused on

* developing the small courtyard immediately outside the classroom

* improving children's independent access to the courtyard

* improving outdoor experiences for less mobile children

* protecting children from wet and damp conditions

* acquisition of resources and equipment that could be easily moved to new premises.

Case study 4.13: Developing outdoor provision despite an uncertain future
St Martin's Pre-school Group, Dover

St Martin's Pre-school Group are a long-established setting based in a church hall with good access to an outdoor area. In recent years the garden has benefited from some improvements, for example a new surface for wheeled toys. The pre-school joined the project with the aim of making further improvements and structural changes to the garden. Sadly, a significant drop in numbers of children attending has made the long-term viability of the pre-school very uncertain. This situation also makes expensive structural changes in the garden a potential waste of time, money and effort. So the staff and committee have been forced to rethink their plans for outdoors.

However, rather than do nothing at all, the pre-school has chosen to concentrate their energy and funds into developing a series of resource boxes for supporting outdoor learning. Some boxes will be developed to further support the kinds of experience that staff know children currently enjoy, for example gardening and investigating. Other boxes will be put together to support outdoor opportunities that staff feel children are not currently experiencing to full advantage, for example den-building and exploration of different weather conditions.

The advantage of this solution is that in the short term children and staff can make better use of their existing outdoor environment, while in the longer term, should the pre-school no longer be viable, the resource boxes can be reallocated to other local pre-schools.

Meeting training needs

Case study 4.14: In-service training for staff
Ditton Church Pre-school

Having officially opened their garden in May, the staff
at Ditton Church Pre-school realised that they would
benefit from further help in developing their role in
supporting children's learning outdoors.
Consequently, they were quick to respond to the
offer of a free workshop advertised in the Space to
Grow project Newsletter.

Outdoor Play Workshops

The Kent Space to Grow
Project aims to help settings
develop more than just the
physical outdoor space. As
we all recognise, even a well-
resourced environment is not
going to be fully effective as a
place for children to play and
learn without enthusiastic
knowledgeable staff who can
support the process. The
review meetings revealed
that for some settings, lower
levels of staff motivation for outdoor play are linked
to a lack of confidence in their own role as outdoor
educators, as well as uncertainty about ways to
promote and support different learning experiences
outdoors. If this strikes a chord.......then read on!

What is in the back of your storage
shed?
Do the children know it is there?
How often is it used?

I am setting aside two weeks from **14–25th
June** to provide a **FREE WORKSHOP on
Outdoor Play** to any project setting who
requests one. I can be flexible about timing,
morning? afternoon? twilight? – even over the
weekend! You just have to get everyone there! I
am happy to tailor each two-hour workshop to your
own requirements. Do you need
specific curriculum ideas, for
example about supporting
mathematical learning outdoors?
Or do you need a more general
session about the adult role? What
about a close look at your existing
equipment to identify new ways of using it,
and to pinpoint any gaps in your
resources? Or would it be helpful to see
some images showing provision in other
settings for discussion and inspiration....?

**If you are
interested, please
call me to book a
date and discuss
your training
needs.**

An informal observation of staff outdoors and a chat with the supervisor indicated the usefulness of a workshop focusing on the staff's role, the curriculum, safety issues and the development of a shared understanding about codes of behaviour. The workshop took place outdoors one afternoon and the tasks and activities concentrated on the following discussion points:

Staff role

Staff were asked to :

* Think about their role indoors

* Identify the kind of demands children made on them as individuals

* Identify the kind of interaction that was taking place between adults and children

Their responses were shared within the workshop session to identify any similarities and differences between the role of adults indoors and outdoors, as a starting point for further discussion.

To promote further discussion staff were asked to discuss a proforma published in *Playing Outside* (Bilton 2004) that identifies the type of demands made by children outdoors.

Next staff were asked to:

* Identify the types of demand they dealt with dealt with most outdoors

* Consider any emerging trends or patterns; for example, why some staff always take children to the toilet, or others tend to be deployed at sedentary activities.

* Identify any changes that need to be made to develop their role as outdoor educators

* Begin to think about how to achieve these changes

Equipment and curriculum issues

Staff were asked to

* Review the current provision outdoors

* Identify any gaps in the existing provision

Outcomes of the discussion:

* No need to replicate exactly the provision indoors and outdoors

* Aim to provide different experiences with same aims/opportunities for learning, e.g. drawing table inside, large-scale painting outside

* Use outdoors to provide experiences that are harder to offer indoors

Next, staff were asked to:

* Work in pairs and use books relating to outdoor play experiences to identify potential activities to address gaps in existing provision

* Share lists of ideas and resources with the staff team

* Identify some key resources

Safety and codes for behaviour

Staff were asked to:

* Discuss and identify key issues and their concerns re safety

* Consider the benefits to children of being experiencing risk and challenge outdoors

Outcomes of the discussion:

* Staff planned to discuss 'codes for behaviour' outdoors with children

* Involve children in developing these codes

* Ensure a shared understanding of what these codes mean in practice

* Staff aim to share reminders about codes in a positive way, i.e. 'we always walk with tools' rather than 'don't run with tools'; 'We always turn the tap off' rather than 'Don't waste water'.

The staff at Ditton Church Pre-school valued the opportunity to discuss these issues and develop a shared understanding of their role as outdoor educators, and their provision and practice outdoors has moved forward as a direct consequence of this training session.

Developing resources

Case study 4.15: Improving the storage and organisation of resources
White Oak Pre-school, Swanley

White Oak Pre-school has a secure accessible garden and both staff and children make good use of it throughout the year. Children are able to take indoor equipment outside to develop their play ideas. However, staff recognised that if the outdoor storage facilities were reorganised and improved a wider range of materials and resources could be provided in the garden to enrich children's outdoor experiences. The acquisition of a large shed with wide double doors has enabled them to achieve this aim. Equipment is stored inside in labelled boxes. Staff agree that the impact of these changes has been very positive:

* children can independently choose and return the materials they need

* the range of outdoor resources has been expanded

* there is enriched potential for outdoor experiences

* there is no conflict of use between children wanting to use resources, such as the tea set, indoors and those who wish to take the same item outdoors.

Developing design solutions

Case study 4.16: Improving children's access to a pond and bog garden
Northfleet Nursery School, Northfleet

Northfleet Nursery School is a maintained nursery in North Kent near Gravesend. It has been established for many years and the staff and children make very good use of the outdoor environment for play and learning across all areas of the curriculum. The focus of their developments as part of the Space to Grow project was the redesign of a small sunken pond

and bog garden. In previous years this feature had been a well-used and important resource; however, a decision was taken to prevent children accessing it following the arrival of a child at the nursery who was unable to recognise the difference between types of surface, i.e. tarmac, grass, water. Consequently, he regularly got wet trying to run across the pond, and had great difficulty understanding the potential hazard in this part of the garden.

Staff recognised that in the longer term a design solution had to be found that allowed for access to the pond for all children. Having cleared the area around the original pond and researched various options with the children, the final solution was the design and installation of a raised pond and bog garden with decked access from all sides. The improved access allowed more children to use the area simultaneously, while the raised design minimised the likelihood of children falling into the water.

Case study 4.17: Overcoming environmental problems
Happy Faces Pre-school, Tonbridge

Staff and children at Happy Faces Pre-school were already making good use of one part of their large outdoor area. However, the remaining space was undeveloped because the land was affected by an underground spring, resulting in extremely boggy conditions throughout the year. The challenge was to find a way of overcoming this problem and allowing children use of the rest of the garden.

Through the determined efforts of a small group of parents the area was slowly transformed. A willow tunnel and other moisture-loving plants were planted to absorb some of the excess water in the soil. A sensory arbour was built with seating and a solar-powered fountain. To allow children to cross and use the boggiest part of the garden, a raised timber decking structure was created in the form of lily pads linked by a bridge.

Prompt sheet 4.1

Involving children in 'Making it happen'

Growing and planting

Preparation

Gather together the tools and resources you will need, for example trowels, pots, plants, seeds, seedlings, watering cans, aprons.

Share stories and factual information about the care of plants with children.

Make labels for plants: laminate children's drawings and writing and attach to lollipop sticks.

Issues to consider

Be attentive to hygiene issues and ensure that children are able to wash their hands after handling soil.

Involve children in the ongoing care of plants and seedlings, for example watering and weeding routines.

Prompt sheet 4.2

Involving children in 'Making it happen'

Creating a sensory area

Preparation

Gather together the resources you will need. Recycle and re-use! Be creative! Local 'scrap schemes' can be a very good source of suitable items.
Consider using:

strips of plastic	twigs and branches
beads	string, wool, rope
CDs	shells
feathers	ribbons
garden netting	plastic bottles
scraps of material	foil food trays.

Issues to consider

The weather will take its toll on children's creations; however, this can be a very good reason for renewing and revitalising the sensory area with new materials at a later date, with a different intake of children.

Prompt sheet 4.3

Involving children in 'Making it happen'

Weaving on fences

Preparation

Gather together the resources you will need. For example, lengths of material, strips of sacking, rope, plastic, barrier tape, grasses, feathers, sticks and twigs.

Issues to consider

The weather will take its toll on children's woven creations; however, this can be a very good reason for renewing and revitalising the fence with new weaving.

Large areas of fencing will take time to complete; consider working on it for short periods over a week. Volunteer help from parents can provide invaluable extra support for the weaving project.

Prompt sheet 4.4

Involving children in 'Making it happen'

Painting murals

Preparation

Gather together the resources and materials you will need; for example, paints, brushes, protective clothing for adults and children.

Have fun!

Issues to consider

You may want to seal children's work afterwards with a varnish to give it a longer-lasting finish.

5 Evaluating and enjoying

Monitor and evaluate the changes outdoors

At each stage of the project it is important to evaluate the progress that has been made:

∗ have the changes improved the outdoor environment?

∗ is it being used in the way that was originally intended? If not, why not?

In Ditton Church Pre-school the ongoing review by staff and children resulted in adaptations to some of the initial plans. For example, children and staff had originally identified planting opportunities as a priority; however, once the two donated planters were in situ it became clear that children valued them as a base for imaginative play. After discussion the plans were changed to allow one planter to be developed as a catalyst for imaginative play. Case study 5.1 outlines further changes that were made at the pre-school following an evaluation once the garden was in full use.

Case study 5.1: Reviewing the use of the garden Ditton Church Pre-school

Having officially opened their new garden at the beginning of May, the staff and children were thoroughly enjoying using it during the summer term. However, after a few weeks it became apparent that some features were not being used in the way that was originally intended and others were not being used much at all. The staff decided to spend time reviewing the children's use of the garden and this review highlighted the following issues:

∗ The bark pit was rarely used.

∗ The digging pit was so popular that staff and parents were having trouble keeping up with the laundering of muddy clothes.

∗ Children were using the shingle path as a source of transportable materials for their trucks, and the presence of shingle all over the grass was making it hard to cut.

∗ The storage and retrieval of wellies was disorganised – staff and children were spending too long looking for a matching pair.

Following the review the garden was reorganised to take account of these issues:

* The bark pit was replaced by earth.

* The shingle path was replaced by the bark and a new area was created where children could play with shingle.

* The flowers in the free-standing planter were repositioned against the fence on the site of the original bark and digging pits.

* The earth in the planter was made available to children for digging.

* The welly storage under the bench was replaced with a transparent storage system that enabled boots to be stored in pairs and easily visible to whoever was searching for a particular set.

This new arrangement in the garden ensured that children still had the same opportunities outdoors but that the management of these experiences was improved.

Aim to involve the whole setting community in evaluating the changes to the outdoor area. There are lots of ways to do this:

* Invite parents in to see the improvements for themselves.

* Encourage children to take their parents on a tour of their favourite places and activities. For more ideas to involve children in evaluating the changes see the Prompt sheets at the end of this chapter.

* Hold events outdoors so that everyone gets a chance to explore the space and comment on the developments that have taken place.

* Put up displays that show the outdoor area changing over time. At Ditton Church Pre-school the project team made a video of their efforts to transform their outdoor area, and it was shown to guests at the event to open the garden.

* Show photographs of children engrossed in outdoor play and display captions alongside each photograph indicating what the children were interested in, what they were saying and doing, and how their play progressed.

* Invite members of the management team to come and see how the space has changed, and talk to staff and children about the new opportunities being provided.

It is easier to maintain enthusiasm for outdoors if everyone can see the types of experience children have, and how they respond to their new outdoor environment. Why not arrange for parents to drop off or collect children from an active outdoor session, rather than from indoors? This will also give the opportunity for parents to observe children playing and for staff to relate the experiences that individual children have been interested and involved in.

Sustain and maintain

Having spent so much time, energy and money improving the outdoor space it is crucial to plan for its sustainability in the longer term. To ensure that it continues to be developed it is essential to think about the maintenance and upkeep of the space and include these costs in the annual budget.

It will also be necessary to discuss and decide upon roles and responsibilities for the area within the staff and management team and, if applicable, among other users.

Consider the following issues:

* Who will carry out safety checks?

* Who will be responsible for ordering replacement items or seasonal items?

* Who will maintain the fences and boundaries to ensure children's safety?

* Have the changes outdoors altered or increased the responsibilities of those staff already involved with its upkeep and maintenance?

* If so, has this been accounted for through a review of the existing job description or maintenance contract?

* How can the children be involved in the care and upkeep of the outdoor space?

* How will organisation, routines and codes of behaviour for outdoors be developed and shared among staff and children?

Enjoying – celebrating success

Whenever an element of the plan has been successfully implemented make sure everyone is aware of the achievement, however large or small. Marking each phase of the project shows the setting community that progress has been made; it also acknowledges the hard work that has been undertaken, and it motivates everyone to make more effort and move forward towards the next stage. There are lots of ways to share what has been achieved at each stage:

* Put up posters
* Send out a newsletter
* Organise a display of 'before' and 'after' photographs

Using CDs to improve the look of alley at Pipsqueaks Day Nursery

Unused alley at Pipsqueaks Day Nursery 'before' the project

* Display children's drawings of the developments alongside captions of their comments
* Display photographs of children using the new area.

Children and staff at Pipsqueaks Day Nursery making good use of the alley

The development of the outdoor space, and the involvement of everyone in that process, is a big accomplishment. Children, their families, staff and the local community will feel the positive benefits of the improvements that have been achieved. So, mark the end of the project with a big celebration:

* Invite a local dignitary to officially open the newly developed space;

* Invite representatives from sponsoring organisations or award bodies;

* Invite the local press.

The Mayor of Tonbridge at Happy Faces Pre-school

* Organise an event for children and their families;

The EDF Energy Team Challenge at Bell Wood Community Primary School

Postman Pat and the local MP opening the garden at Ditton Church Pre-school

What happens next?

In July 2005 the Kent 'Space to Grow' Project reached its final stages. The 22 settings involved have moved a long way towards achieving the key aims of the project: to improve children's access to and use of outdoors, to enhance the quality of children's experiences outdoors, and to increase practitioner confidence, motivation and enthusiasm for outdoor learning. The settings involved in the project were asked to evaluate what they had learnt through their participation, and identify what they would do differently another time. Table 5.1 highlights these comments and will be of significant interest to anyone considering a similar undertaking.

The project has been full of challenges and obstacles that have been met with determination and persistence by the settings involved. All their hard work has now paid off and both children and staff are benefiting from an enriched outdoor curriculum. Many settings have noted the positive impact that changing and developing the use of the outdoor learning environment has on the indoor environment. Staff report lower levels of noise indoors, higher levels of concentration, and calmer, more purposeful play amongst children. Similarly, having discovered that learning outdoors can be successfully supported through activities that are initiated and led by children, some practitioners are questioning whether a similar approach could be used indoors. Consequently, several settings have begun to review their planning techniques. Staff are moving away from plans that are based round a topic or theme, and are embracing a planning approach that has the child at its centre and uses children's current interests and enthusiasms to provide direction and focus for the interaction, resources and experiences that are offered.

Learning through Landscapes has provided direct support for two years to a small representative selection of early years settings across Kent through the Space to Grow project. The achievements of the project have already influenced the support and materials that Learning through Landscapes provides to other early years settings through membership of *Early Years Outdoors*, conferences and training events, facilitation resources and case studies. It is anticipated that the positive impact of the project will continue and, through the publication of this book, will now be disseminated to a much wider audience across Kent and beyond.

Page 90 has more information about Learning through Landscapes and *Early Years Outdoors*.

Table 5.1 Evaluating what has been learnt through the project

What have you learnt?	What would you do differently?
* Children have a lot to offer us – ideas, enthusiasm * The project has strengthened bonds between staff and parents * The use of outdoors changes the use of indoors * Outdoors has a positive impact on learning and children's behaviour * Networking with others is vital * Involving others is essential * To start from what you have and develop it * To seek donations – don't be embarrassed to ask for what you want	* Plan project thoroughly – don't rush in * Manage time spent on the project carefully * Delegate * Look for ways to combine initiatives and work together * Tell people about the project * Keep people informed throughout the project * Use knowledge and observation of children to inform the project * Involve children throughout the project * Take account of seasonal factors when planning the outdoor space * Give external contractors a very specific brief and closely supervise their work * Record the process – for funding bids, external regulatory bodies

Prompt sheet 5.1

Involving children in 'Evaluating and enjoying'

Surveying the existing space: Tours (see Clark and Moss 2005: 37–9)

When to use this activity

Useful technique for

* active children who like to be on the move
* identifying emerging favourite spaces
* surveying new or changed features in the environment
* identifying new features, items or activities of importance to the child
* reviewing the space before and after any developments (see 'Getting started', Prompt sheet 2.1).

Use this activity to review and build up information about what children like to do outdoors following the implementation of the planned changes.

Preparation and resources

Offer children a variety of methods for recording their views during the tour. Options could include

* cameras
* clipboards, pencils and paper
* audio or video tape recorders
* dictaphone.

Gathering the information

Individual children take an adult on a tour of the outdoor space. They can be given control of the route of the tour and how their preferences are recorded during the tour, and how they will be documented later.

Ask open questions, such as 'What happens now in this part of the garden?'

Making sense of the information

Invite children to share their thoughts with other children or staff. Looking at the photographs, drawings or recordings will promote further discussion about the newly developed space and ensure that staff draw an accurate conclusion about children's views.

Issues to consider

Keep an open mind and try not to make assumptions about the information children provide. For example, for some children the importance of particular areas of the garden is strongly linked to whether or not it is associated with social interaction with friends rather than to the new equipment or features that are sited there. Also, an initial evaluation of children's views about their new space is likely to be influenced by the very newness of the space or feature, i.e. some children may be particularly drawn to it because of the novelty, while others may actively avoid it until they feel more accustomed to it.

Prompt sheet 5.2

Involving children in 'Evaluating and enjoying'

Surveying the space: Tours with an intermediary, such as a puppet or soft toy

When to use this activity

Useful technique for

* identifying the impact of changes and new features

* gathering children's perspectives on the new developments

* reviewing the space before and after any developments (see 'Getting started', Prompt sheet 2.3)

* identifying future priorities

* identifying emerging favourite and important places

* children under three years old

* children with limited or undeveloped communication skills.

Use this activity to build up detailed information about what children feel about their newly developed outdoor space. The use of an intermediary, such as a named puppet or soft toy, can provide a focus for the survey with very young children. It is also a useful technique if the adult conducting the survey is not well known to the children; they may be reluctant to share their thoughts with an unfamiliar adult but will be happy to talk to the toy. Alternatively, very young children with a limited vocabulary or those with communication difficulties can use the soft toy to show an adult what they like or dislike in different parts of the garden.
(See Clark and Moss 2005: 102)

Preparation and resources

Introduce the puppet or toy, or use one that is already known to the children. It is easier if the puppet has a name for children and adults to refer to it by, for example 'Bertie'.

Consider taking photographs as a record of the tour findings and a catalyst for further discussions among staff and children.

Offer children some options for recording their thoughts, for example through drawings, photographs or tape recordings.

Gathering the information

Individual children take 'Bertie' and an adult on a tour of the outdoor space. Either allow children to choose the route of the tour or ask them to show 'Bertie' where particular experiences take place.

Ask open questions, such as 'Can you show/tell Bertie what happens now in this part of the garden?' or 'If Bertie wanted to hide in the garden where would he go?'

Making sense of the information

Invite the children involved in the tour to share their thoughts with other children or staff. Create a book using photographs or children's drawings to promote further discussion about the space. Create a display using 'Bertie' and captioned photographs that identify what children think he could do in each part of the garden.

Issues to consider

Keep an open mind; children's perspectives on the best place for Bertie to go for particular experiences may differ from the adult view and from the original plans for the space.

The use of an intermediary can enable children to open up about more sensitive issues, such as why they have strong preferences for, or an aversion to particular parts of the garden. These insights will need careful consideration by everyone involved in reviewing the achievements of the project and identifying priorities for any further developments.

Prompt sheet 5.3

Involving children in 'Evaluating and enjoying'

Finding out how children feel about the newly developed outdoor environment: happy tokens

When to use this activity

Useful technique for

* active children who like to be on the move

* identifying children's preferences in the new environment

* gathering opinions about new features in the environment

* identifying new features, items or activities of emerging importance to the child

* reviewing how children feel about the space before and after any developments (see 'Getting started', Prompt sheet 2.5).

Preparation and resources

Gather together several containers and some tokens. The tokens can be anything that is in plentiful supply, for example bricks, beads, buttons. However, take care that the size of the token does not represent a choking hazard to very young children.

Label the containers with a happy or sad face and a note of where they are to be sited. Place them in pairs around the outdoor area in key spots, for example by new features or changed spaces.

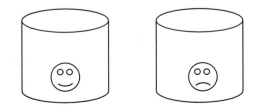

Gathering the information

Encourage children who visit each area to collect a token and drop it into the pot with the face that represents how they feel about the new feature or changed space.

Making sense of the information

By counting the number of tokens in each pot it will be easy to establish emerging preferences for particular areas of the garden. This may confirm the success of the original plans or may provide unforeseen problems. Children can help to count and collate the information onto a summary sheet.

Issues to consider

Some children may not have a strong preference for a particular area. Therefore it may be appropriate to introduce a third pot labelled with a neutral expression to allow these children to express their viewpoint.

It is possible to determine preferences linked to gender or age by giving children preordained tokens; for example, by using a particular colour or shape of token for boys/girls, or for children under/over three years old. This will provide useful additional details that can be used to inform any further developments.

Prompt sheet 5.4

Involving children in 'Evaluating and enjoying'

Finding out how children feel about the improvements to their outdoor environment: cheer rating

When to use this activity

Useful technique for

* active children who like to be on the move

* identifying children's preferences in the newly developed environment

* reviewing the space before and after any developments (see 'Getting started', Prompt sheet 2.6).

Preparation and resources

This activity needs little preparation or resources. It is a very useful evaluative activity that can be used to get children familar with the process of giving an opinion on aspects of their new outdoor environment. Children express their preferences and levels of enthusiasm for different parts of the garden by cheering in each area. A tape recorder is a useful way to record children's responses.

Gathering the information

Having explained the activity to the children, visit each part of the garden with a small group and encourage them to cheer – loudly or quietly according to how they feel about the space. Consider using a tape recorder to document children's responses. Remember to mention on tape where each cheer takes place to help make sense of the recording afterwards.

Making sense of the information

It will be possible to form a general view about how children feel about the developments, based on their cheer responses. This may confirm the view of adults in the setting or may offer new perspectives.

Issues to consider

This activity does not reveal accurate measurable information; however, it is fun and it will provide a broad overview about how children feel.

Resources and contacts

For further information about Learning through Landscapes' work with schools and early years settings please contact:

Learning through Landscapes
3rd Floor
Southside Offices
The Law Courts,
Winchester SO23 9DL.
Tel: 01962 845811.
Email: eyo@ltl.org.uk
www.ltl.org.uk

Learning through Landscapes' membership benefit: Site Visit. Materials developed as part of Learning through Landscapes' Developmental Site Visit Service provided a valuable source of information and a structure for the organisation of this book.

National Children's Bureau (www.ncb.org.uk)

© Learning through Landscapes

Early Years Outdoors is Learning through Landscapes' support service for all early years practitioners. Regular mailings keep practitioners in touch with the latest news and developments, as well as providing information and advice about the development of outdoor spaces as high-quality learning environments. Further information about *Early Years Outdoors* can be obtained by contacting LtL the above address or logging on to the website.

Bibliography

BILTON, HELEN (2005) *Playing Outisde: Activities, Ideas and Inspiration for the Early Years*. London: David Fulton Publishers.

CLARK, ALISON (2004) *Why and How We Listen to Young Children*. Listening as a Way of Life series. London: National Children's Bureau.

CLARK, ALISON AND MOSS, PETER (2005) *Listening to Young Children: The Mosaic Approach*. London: National Children's Bureau. ISBN 1-90099-062-8

CLARK, ALISON AND MOSS, PETER (2005) *Spaces to Play: More Listening to Young Children Using the Mosaic Approach*. London: National Children's Bureau. ISBN 1-904787-43-6

DICKINS, MARY (2004) *Listening to Young Disabled Children*. Listening as a Way of Life series. London: National Children's Bureau.

DICKINS, MARY, EMERSON, SU AND GORDON-SMITH, PAT (2004) *Starting with Choice: Inclusive Strategies for Consulting with Young Children*. Save the Children Fund. ISBN 1-84187-085-4.

FAJERMAN, LINA AND SUTTON, FAYE (2000) *Children as Partners in Planning*. Save the Children Fund. ISBN 1-84187-031-5

KINNEY, LINDA AND MCCABE, JERRY (2001) *Children as Partners: a Guide to Consulting with Very Young Children and Empowering them to Participate Effectively*. Stirling Council. (Available from Children's Services, Stirling Council, Viewforth, Stirling FK8 2ET.)

LINDON, JENNIE (2003) *Too Safe for their Own Good? Helping Children Learn about Risk and Life Skills*. London: National Children's Bureau.

Measuring Success: A Guide to Evaluating School Grounds Projects (2004). Learning through Landscapes. ISBN 1-87286-532-1. (Includes ideas for involving children of all ages in the evaluation of their grounds. Some of the ideas appropriate to children under five have been included in this publication.)

OUVRY, MARJORIE (2003) *Exercising Muscles and Minds: Outdoor Play and the Early Years Curriculum*. London: NCB Books. ISBN 1-904787-01-0

RICH, DIANE (2004) *Listening to Babies*. Listening as a Way of Life series. London: National Children's Bureau.